Ride o[n]

C000182758

BIG MILE CYCLING

SEAN CONWAY

Big Mile Cycling
Copyright © Sean Conway 2019
www.SeanConway.com

Sean Conway has asserted his right to be identified as
the author of this Work in accordance with the
Copyright, Design and Patent Act 1988

First published in 2019

Mortimer Lion Publishing
www.MortimerLion.co.uk

Front cover photo by: Caroline Conway
Back cover photo: @ospreyimagery

Edited by
Melanie Spratley
Zen Hoppé
Babette Pinder

ISBN 978-0-9574497-6-3

Other books by Sean

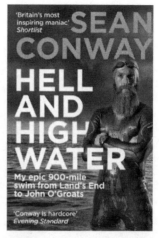

For
Mike and Lee

The Ultra-Cyclist - Someone who cycles a very long way which results in them being mostly cold, wet, very hungry and in a lot of pain, and then they do it again.
Anonymous

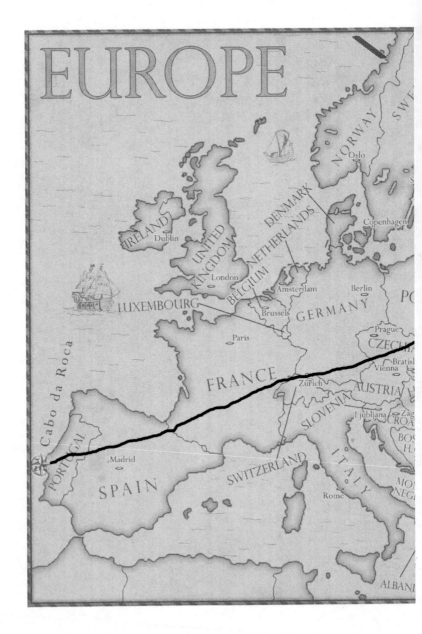

FINLAND
Helsinki
SWEDEN
Stockholm
Tallinn ESTONIA
Riga
LATVIA
LITHU-ANIA
Vilnius
Minsk
BELARUS
Warsaw
POLAND
Kiev
UKRAINE
SLOVAKIA
HUNGARY
Budapest
CROATIA
Zagreb
Beograd
SERBIA
BOSNIA & H.G.
Sarajevo
ROMANIA
Bucuresti
MOLDOVA
KOSOVO
MONTENEGRO
Tirana
Skopje
BULGARIA
Sofia
GREECE
Athens
MACEDONIA
Istanbul
TURKEY
RUSSIA
Moscow
Ufa
GEORGIA
Tbilisi

9

PROLOGUE

The internet seems to suggests that the definition of ultra cycling is anything more than 100 miles. Well that's just ridiculous. Only 100 miles. I have friends who can run 100 miles. If ultra-cycling is only 100 miles then what I've been captivated by for the last decade, and others going back more than a century, is bigger than that, much bigger. It's thousands and thousands of miles, on two wheels, and at lightning pace. This, for me, is what real ultra-cycling really is. The pursuit of chasing big miles, fast. For the purpose of distinction between the seemingly short definition of ultra-cycling, I've decided to call what really inspires me, big mile cycling.

There is something about big mile cycling that is hard to explain. Mileage, sleep strategies, nutrition, hydration, fatigue, all taking centre stage in your mind in an effort to cycle just a few miles further each day than everyone else. Your legs like iron pistons hammering down towards the road with precision and power, your mind, turning to survival mode where nothing else matters in the world. Every bit of available brain space allocated to one task and one task only, keeping your legs moving round and round.

Being a big mile cyclist means different things to different people. For me though, I only felt I could claim that title if I had a world record to my name. This is my story of big mile cycling.

PART ONE — THE BEGINNING

'So what bike are you using Mike?' asked Richard, a fellow Global Bike Race competitor in a comment on Facebook, a fairly obvious opportunity to find out as much as he could about who he was up against. There were 8 other riders also in the race, most of whom he had little concern for, but who he had a great deal of concern for was the unassuming master of miles, Mr Mike Hall. Mike was by far the most acclaimed of the 9 competitors who had signed up to the inaugural 2012 bike race around the globe. I was one of them, even though at the time this was going on, I still didn't have a bike.

'A black one,' replied Mike. You could just imagine the smirk on his face as he wrote that. This was my first ever encounter with Mike and I immediately started to find out a bit more about him.

Mike was born nearly 2 months after me all the way back in 1981. So, we were for all intents and purposes, the same age. He had however a far greater CV when it came to long distance cycling. Before this race he'd achieved highest rookie position in the 2011 Tour Divide, a race he would go on to win twice, breaking the course record in 2016. He also featured heavily on podiums in 24-hour MTB races. He was a machine. As I discovered more about Mike I couldn't help but feel mixed emotions. On the one hand I became almost a fan-boy, but on the other hand he was my competition for the round the world race and I needed to 'hate' him if you know what I mean. But I figured I'd leave the hate until race time because, well, on paper the quiet Yorkshireman was probably going to kick my ass in this round the world race, but that in itself was just the fuel I needed to keep up with my 40 hours a week training programme.

This was my first real inclusion into the world of big mile cycling. Up until a few months previously I had been nothing more than a mildly interested bystander, watching and observing the likes of Mark Beaumont and Al Humphreys cycle a long, long way, regarding them in the same light as astronauts and rocket scientists – 'it's not something I am able to be a part of', I often thought to myself whenever I saw or heard of anyone doing these sorts of challenges. These folks, these super humans, were just of another class, often literally, than I was and I never dreamed it possible to even think I could be one of them.

That all changed, initially with just a passing 'maybe I could?' after I cycled Land's End to John O'Groats back in 2008, but the idea pretty quickly died a death when it took me 25 days to complete the ride. When I reached

John O'Groats, I finished at the same time as a couple in their late 60's who did it in 14 days. I was a bit depressed at my lack of physical ability, and reinforcing my belief that I certainly wasn't 'one of those people', I returned to London, got caught up in the perils of 'just existing' and I didn't cycle again for another 3 years.

My second wave of enthusiasm for long distance cycling came with noticeably more gusto, and with hindsight, the completely and utterly deluded thought that; 'Maybe I really could actually ride a bike a very long way and ride it fast? Maybe?' This came when I had an early mid-life crisis at the age of 30. I was pretty miserable in my un-achieving life so sold my school portrait photography business for £1. Yes, I was that guy who would go into schools (nursery schools at that), take photos of 100 (often crying) babies and then try and flog the photos to the parents for exorbitant prices. Turns out parents love to buy these photos. Business was great. My wellbeing however was not. So I gave it all up for that famous Jersey one-pound note. Famous only to me because it's been on my desk, slowly gathering dust in its frame, a frame that actually cost me four times as much as I sold my business for, £4, thus making the sale of Lifepix Photography probably the worst business deal in the history of terrible business deals. That framed quid does, however, remind me how not to live life - purely for the money.

So, at the age of 30, with no real cycling experience, and minus £3 to my name, it seemed completely reasonable to try and beat a fairly competent Yorkshireman in a cycling race around the world. 'Fake it until you make it' was something I had been told once. I was most certainly doing just that.

Now, a few months on, I was in too deep to pull out. I had a big training plan, a flat in London I couldn't afford to rent any longer so had to leave anyway, and a donations page already set up raising money for a solar charity in Africa that already had £58 in it from friends and family supporting my early mid-life crisis, or trying to get rid of me. Either way, I was here now, trawling through Mike Hall and Richard Dunnet's Facebook page to try and find out anything about what they were up to which may give me any sort of advantage.

Still being a complete rookie, I soon realised I was over sharing my entire training programme, something I quickly learned how to manage. Never post your big rides online. Always post the smaller rides where you only do 150 miles and say how huge it was, and how tired you are but feeling on top of your game. Big mile cycling isn't all about fitness. There are many other aspects that cyclists needs to look into. Food, water, sleep, lack of sleep, navigation, kit, searching towns along the route and finding out when and what time various shops that you may need will be open or closed. It's more than just being able to cycle quickly. When you decide you want to become a big mile cyclist, you're almost joining a cult, a cult that will take over your life and spread across into everything you do. You may find that you prefer using a cut-in-half toothbrush at home. You may find yourself sleeping in your sleeping bag on the floor of your kitchen. You'll even wear all your lycra around the house all day. You'll live, eat, breathe cogs and chains and you'll feel on top of the world for it. It's just a shame it took me over 3 decades to realise just how much I loved it.

Cycling Land's End to John O'Groats in 2008

Before my early mid-life crisis, I had a largely vague relationship with cycling. I far preferred my little skateboard and got quite good at it in my younger years. My first memory of being on a bike was in 1986. I was 5 years old. I was bombing down a gravel hill with the naïve confidence all children possess, on a BMX that only had front brakes. The impending corner at the bottom of the hill resulted in me pulling the front brake, too hard of course, being catapulted over the handle bars and head-butting the road. A trickle of blood ran down my face and into my mouth. I remember it being warm and tasting weird, probably the first time I had ever tasted blood. I got up in somewhat of a daze, with mild concussion no doubt, and pushed my bike back home. I don't have many memories cycling after that, and for the next decade I actually had a bump on my forehead and my mother joked that I still had a stone stuck in there. Looking back now I probably fractured my skull and what I was feeling was broken bone.

Other than a few BMX rides around the garden, it wasn't until 1996 when I was 15 years old, that I got on a proper bicycle. I lived on a sugar cane farm on the east coast of South Africa near a small town called Stanger with my mum and step-father, Doug, who was the accountant for the farm.

Just below our house was the start of a brand spanking new motorway, with the most perfect blacktop a cyclist could ever wish for running 30 miles north from our house, but, and this happens a lot in Africa, they had run out of money to complete the last few miles so the motorway lay abandoned for years, blocked up by huge boulders to stop cars driving up it. Other than a few rogue taxis it was traffic-free, a cyclist's dream. I remember going out with Doug on his vintage steel bike and doing a 2-hour loop over the Tugela River, up to the bridge near the farm with the water silos and then back again. It was a tough ride for my little legs as I watched Doug beast it up the hill ahead of me and wait at the top. I was slow but didn't mind it at the time. I just liked the feeling of wind passing my ears and the knowledge that I could get somewhere, that ordinarily we would drive too, by just using my own two legs.

In every other cyclist's biography book this is the part where they say; 'I was hooked', but the truth is I wasn't. At best I was mildly amused by the idea of cycling. You must remember I was living in a part of South Africa where crime was quite ferocious, and it wasn't uncommon for people to be murdered for their bicycle. This very much limited where and when I, or anyone else for that matter, could have cycled safely. I was also 15 years old, a little too set in my teenage ways to realise the romance of cycling, caught up instead in the throes of being a spotty ginger adolescent, high school, exams, and trying not to be murdered of course. That said I still went to the local bike shop and mum bought me a Raleigh hardtail mountain bike with front suspension for the grand total of 500 Rand, the equivalent of about £30 in today's money. My experience with cycling then took another downhill turn when, back at school, I was trying to show off in front of a group of girls from a nearby school who had come to use our fields for hockey practice. I thought I'd try and do a wheelie near a rugby ball, and then kick it while still on the bike, hoping it would go over the posts. I gave a huge push on the pedals while pulling up on the handlebars with all the effort I could muster. The front wheel lifted off the ground, and then fell back down almost immediately, my wheelie lasting all of about 0.7 seconds. Still determined to reclaim my dignity I cycled right past the rugby ball and gave it the biggest kick of my life. Instead of the world's best place kick, the ball shanked off the inside of my right foot and got stuck between the rear of my front wheel and the frame. I immediately went head first over the handlebars to the jeers and uproars of the girls, all potential suiters of course. Besides bending the forks, my £30 bicycle became the source of immense embarrassment whenever I saw it, my friends constantly reminding me of that infamous moment and how it was very likely I'd never ever find a girlfriend because of it. Those jeers are still as clear as day in my mind as I write this. So, with my seemingly subconscious desire to fly over handlebars and lifelong singledom at stake, I put my bike away. I didn't cycle again for another decade.

Although I wasn't an avid cyclist as a youngster, or even a young adult, I was however interested in other people cycling, much like I am interested in astronauts, and racing car drivers. This interest didn't extend towards professional cycling and it's only been in the last 5 years that I've followed Le Tour de France. I just couldn't quite find any inspiration in a peloton of 'millionaire' cyclists all drugged up, fully supported, only cycling 130 miles a day. It just didn't peak my interest. Those were my early thoughts and I must admit I'm far less cynical and definitely more of a dreamer nowadays when I watch professional bike racing and for the most part I now choose to think that riders today are clean and that makes me feel better, even if may not be true, but I hope it is.

What I was far more interested in were the people who decided, for no real fame or glory, other than maybe to get a few free pints down the pub, to get on their bike and just ride. Mike Hall said something during the TransAm bike race (which he won) in the film *Inspired to Ride*, which I will never forget. He had just cycled through the night and didn't know what day it was, thinking it was a Thursday (it was probably Saturday), he pulled into a service station and was asked how he was feeling. He smiled and replied 'You can't take yourself too seriously. It's only riding bikes at the end of the day.'

That really stuck with me and is something I always think about, and often question. Was only riding your bike enough? I loved the fact that it's all Mike, and so many others before him, wanted to do, just ride their bikes.

I preferred my skateboard to my bike

The real story of big mile cycling, for me anyway, started way back on 22nd April 1884 with a gentleman called Thomas Stevens. Mr Stevens, a mine worker by trade, decided he'd take the fairly new mechanical invention, called the Penny-Farthing (also known as an Ordinary), around the world. Living in a time of unparalleled exploration, Mr Stevens set off from San Francisco and spent the next $2^{1/2}$ years cycling 13,500 miles across the northern hemisphere. I have no doubt that there may have been other people who had also done some big miles on a bicycle prior to Mr Stevens but this ride certainly captured people's imagination and he'd have upwards of 500 people seeing him off from places like San Francisco, Liverpool and London.

Mr Stevens' ride around the world was truly incredible. He had to walk a third of it because, well, if any of you have managed to actually cycle a Penny-Farthing will know anything above a 5% gradient uphill is too steep and any downhill becomes a kamikaze suicide endeavour as the pedals take on a mind of their own, becoming lethal spinning ankle breakers.

The other reason I've become somewhat of an admirer of Stevens was because he also spent time looking for explorer Henry Morton Stanley, while Stanley was looking for fellow explorer David Livingstone who'd gone AWOL in Africa. Livingstone was identified as the catalyst for the scramble for Africa, something my English and Irish family were caught up in in the early 20th Century, which is why I was born in Zimbabwe. I kind of like that in some very small way, Stevens and I were linked, no more so than every other British and Irish colonial African, of which there are millions, but none the less, it was an important link for me anyway.

7 years passed from when Mr Stevens' mammoth bike ride ended when a wager was set that no woman could cycle around the world in under 15 months. Of course, this created an uproar and rightly so. One woman decided to take on the wager. Her name was Annie Cohen Kopchovsky but due to the difficulties of being Jewish on such a ride she changed her name to Annie Londonderry, named after her first main sponsor, Londonderry Lithia Spring Water. Some say she pioneered what now seems normal in the sports world by selling logo space on her clothing to fund the trip. Although there were large portions of the ride where she took trains and ferries (the people who set the wager stupidly never set a minimum distance to cycle) she still went around the world with her bike in a time where such things were just not 'the done thing' for a lady to do.

Fast-forward 113 years and I too had finally decided to do my own epic bike ride. It was 2008 and I had decided to cycle the length of Britain. Like the three previous years, I had taken one month off to go travelling. 30 glorious days of hedonistic self-fulfilment. Being a self-employed photographer allowed me to do this, as long as I did it in the winter when most people didn't actually want their photo taken. In 2006 I had gone back to South Africa to visit family. In 2007 I went traveling through India, Nepal and Tibet and in 2008 I wanted to do something different, a challenge of sorts. Various ideas came to mind but most were woefully over-ambitious or just too expensive. It wasn't until one evening as I sat with my flatmate Rob when he asked me if I'd ever been to Scotland.

'Edinburgh,' I replied.

'No, real Scotland?' he said somewhat angrily.

'No I haven't,' I replied embarrassingly.

'What about the Lake District?'

'No.'

'Yorkshire Dales?'

'Nope.'

'Wales? Surely you've been to Wales mate?' He said.

'Cardiff,' I said with my head hung low.

Rob went on to mention all parts of beautiful Britain I hadn't even heard of. It was then the idea was born. I'd cycle the iconic Land's End to John O'Groats.

Once I had decided, and it's amazing how your brain suddenly recalls something it hasn't thought about in years, I remembered that some time ago there had been a chap who broke the record for this route. His name was Gethin Butler and he managed the near on 900-mile ride in 44 hours. Incredible! In fact, as I write this in 2018 his record just been beaten by Michael Broadwith in a time of 43 hours and 25 minutes. Gethin had held the record for nearly two decades.

It blew my mind when I originally found out about the LEJOG record and now that I was going to follow in his footsteps, albeit much slower, it was blowing my mind all over again. I immediately went on eBay and bought the first touring bike I saw for under £300 (my budget). It landed up being a 62cm sized frame. If any of you have met me you'll know I'm rather short. I actually ride a 52cm frame so you can imagine how ridiculous I looked on this incredibly oversized bicycle.

It was the beginning of April with snow still forecasted when I started my ride from Land's End. It was windy and cold most of the time but I pushed on, camping in deserted campsites, and exploring anywhere and everywhere that was remotely on my route. Back in 2008 there were no smart phones so one of my 5 panniers was full of paper things. I had an AA road map book with all the pages I may not need, like Essex and Kent, torn out. I had a camping guide book. I had a British Lonely Planet, which by the way is excellent and bigger than the one for India. Lastly, I had an actual book. Bryce Courtney's – The Power of One, also, a hefty size. All those books are now within your phone, which in a way is kind of sad.

Life on the road was brilliant and divided into 5 mile per hour segments. 20-30 miles in the morning. Find something fun to explore like a museum or monument, and then another 20-30 miles in the afternoon where I'd find a pub, meet some locals, and inquire about a suitable campsite for the night. I went to Stonehenge, diverted into Wales, climbed Ben Nevis and eventually, 25 days later, reached John O'Groats, a lot hairier, skinnier and grubbier but the happiest I have ever been in my life.

Again, as in every other cyclist's book, at the end of my adventure and the first proper bike ride where I didn't fall over my handlebars, I should have been hooked, and I very nearly was. I remember sitting at John O'Groats thinking, I wish there was more land, I just don't want to stop cycling and at that moment I saw the ferry to Orkney so I raced to catch it and did in fact carry on north for another 4 days of island hopping. 5 days later on the 9-hour train back to London I remember promising myself that I would most definitely, without any doubt, do much, much more cycling.

Cycling the length of Britain was the best thing I had

Enjoying a leisurely morning before a day's cycling

ever done and although my daily mileage was dismal, 60 miles at the most, it ignited a fire inside me. The seed for becoming a real big mile cyclist had been planted. Excitedly I returned back to my dingy flat, cleaned my bike (which I had even named Valerie) ready for the next adventure and put her in the shed, where she stayed for the next 3 years. Although the seed had been planted, it seemed I didn't know what fertiliser to use. There just seemed to be something missing, some magical ingredient that I needed to keep on cycling but I just didn't have a clue what it should be.

A few months before I cycled the length of Britain, someone else had just completed a ride that some say reignited the world of long distant cycling records. His name was Mark Beaumont and he had just broken the record for round the world cycling. Strangely, I somehow missed Mark's achievement when it happened but became aware and excited by it a few months later once I had completed LEJOG. By the looks of things, we had very similar 5 pannier setups, (sleek lightweight saddle and frame bags and the term bikepacking hadn't been invented yet) but the idea of doing over 100 miles per day simply seemed impossible.

Although Mark's 2008 record of 194 days was good, averaging 100 miles per day, it was still far off what people were cycling nearly a century before him. Big mile cycling has had its moments of popularity in the past. After Stevens' round the world ride, there seemed to be a lull in people going for the global challenge. There was a far more admirable challenge in fashion back in the 20s and 30's but we'll get onto that later. In the 80's there was a chap called Nick Sanders who set the first round the world record of 138 days. Not happy with that, he went back and did it again in 79 days a few years later. It must be said that back then the distance was only 13,000 miles and not the 18,000 it is today. Even so Nick's average pace of just above 160 miles per day was far higher than Mark's or anyone else doing serious miles at the beginning of this century. I can safely say this without offending Mark because 10 years later Mark would go on to do one of the most impressive big mile bike rides the world has ever seen.

In 1984 Nick also went on to break the record for cycling a lap of Britain. He completed his 4,800 mile ride in 21 days, a record that still stands to this day. To prepare for the British lap record Nick actually went and did the lap. His training ride was to do one lap and then the second lap would be the record. He was a machine.

I was intrigued by Nick's success back in the 80s so I called him to ask if he had any competitors, anyone else gunning for the big records, the big miles.

'Um, I can't really remember,' he said a bit vaguely.

'There were these two cousins, Richard and Nicholas Crane. They were doing some big miles but not the records. I seem to have been the only one silly enough back in those days,' he laughed.

It's also interesting to discover that these huge achievements have somewhat faded in Nick's mind. A few years ago I too had contemplated the round Britain record and wanted to find out where Nick had started his ride.

'Well I tell you, I can't quite remember, I think it was Blackpool. I don't know why I chose Blackpool but it must have been for a good reason,' he said as if he hadn't thought about it for years.

'I'm almost certain I went clockwise,' he continued.

'Because I remember thinking that if I cycled on the left-hand side of the road I would have been on the most outer edge of Britain and therefore done a better job of it. Had I gone counter-clockwise I would have been on the inside lane and we couldn't have that now could we,' he joked.

Nick was also the one who told me to take many photos when I cycled around the world because the memories, however grand and awesome they seem at the time, do fade. Our conversations were testament to that.

Nick sadly stopped cycling and got into motor biking and actually broke the round the world motorbike record which he did in 19 days, a record that Guinness wouldn't give him as they said he would have broken the speed limit to achieve it. With Nick out of the cycling world, there seemed to be another lull in big mile cycling. Yes, there had been a few people doing significant rides here and there but nothing that grabbed people's attention.

Cycling with Mark Beaumont in Scotland

That all changed with Mark Beaumont's ride in 2008. His ride caught the imagination of almost every cyclist in Britain who dreamed of just getting on their bike and not getting off for a very long time. The floodgates had been opened and soon there were head to head attempts as people tried, and succeeded to break Mark's record. It was a very exciting time for big mile cycling indeed. There seemed to be a new enthusiasm and the cult of dirty, unkept, cyclists was reborn with one goal in mind, to ride bikes far, and fast.

In 2009 a bearded gent called James Bowthorpe broke Mark's record and brought it down to 176 days but for some reason his attempt got largely overlooked even though he nearly got kidnapped in Iran. Then Julian Sayarer brought the record down to 169 days. Neither of their records were submitted to Guinness.

Then in 2010 excitement soon turned to Vin Cox and Alan Bate who were both going for it at the same time. Alan doing a partially supported ride, which is allowed, and Vin unsupported. Guinness don't differentiate between the two, you can choose to go supported or self-supported but for the most part people choose the latter as it's more exciting and a lot less expensive. Vin actually started his ride unaware that Alan's supported attempt was going to start a month into his ride. Vin got all the way to Bangkok before Alan (who coincidentally lived in Bangkok) began his ride. Alan was always going to beat Vin but with such a head start and similar mileage for the first part Vin soon forgot about Alan's ride knowing he was going to complete the ride before him, and continued on having the adventure he had dreamt of. In fact, Vin, so bombarded by trolls and online

31

comments from Alan's tribe of supporters, actually told everyone to stop talking about it as it was taking away from his ride. I have no doubt Alan was getting similar messages from Vin's tribe. The 'supported versus self-supported' was always going to polarise opinions.

Vin then made a grave error in route calculations. Analysing Australian wind roses (a circular diagram showing the wind's average speed and direction) wrongly he chose to cycle Darwin down to Sydney. He read the wind roses as having a tailwind the whole way when in fact he had a killer headwind. Vin accounts for averaging around 8 mile per hour for over 2,000 miles. Alan did the more common southern route and flew across gaining days on Vin.

Still none the wiser how close things were going to be Vin carried on unaware of Alan's progress. It wasn't until he was in America when he was cycling along and his phone rang. It was his sister. I've spoken to Vin about this and he recounts the story.

'Hey Viv,' he answered.

'Hey Vin. Now I know you said you don't want us to talk about Alan . . .'

'You're right, I don't,' he butted in.

'Well, the thing is. He has been doing some big miles while supported and at the going rate he will finish his ride a few days before you finish.'

I can just imagine what Vin was thinking. Years of planning, training and fundraising, all for nothing because a fully supported rider was going to get to the finish line a few days before him.

'So you better pull your finger out and start cycling proper,' she said.

I would have been heartbroken but Vin took it in his stride and said it gave him the motivation to push harder. Vin stepped up a few gears, taking bigger risks, doing longer days, cycling well into the night. He had to get to the end before Alan. His mileage went up dramatically from around 120 miles to 150 miles per day. It was tight and a week before they were both due to finish it was neck and neck. Vin then had another hurdle. It looked like his route was nearly 2 days longer than it needed to be. He was due to cycle more than the 18,000 miles. 226 miles more. There was a real chance that he may complete the record distance (18,000 miles) before Alan, but not yet be back at the start/finish line. That would just add salt to the already bitter wound.

Alan found out about this and realised it would be a real rubbish thing to do so slowed down a little. He was still trying to get Guinness to give him a separate 'supported' record but if they decided it was the same one he felt it unfair to beat an unsupported rider in that way. Vin came in a few days before Alan and the race was over. Vin got the record officially off Mark Beaumont, unofficially off Julian Sayarer in a time of 163 days. Alan's time was 125 days but it took nearly 2 years before Guinness eventually gave him the record deciding in the end there is no distinction between supported and self-supported, even though Alan had pleaded for it.

In the meantime, while Guinness put Alan's claim at the bottom of their priority pile in favour of deciding how heavy each of the three lemons needs to be in the 'Fastest time to peel and eat three lemons' record, Vin was on another mission. Aware that his official record could be beaten, he decided to put on the world's first ever self-supported Global Bicycle Race and invited people to take the record off him. The idea was simple.

'If anyone wants to try and break my record, why don't you all start at the same time, on the same day and make it a race,' he announced.

'Everyone will be tracked online and each rider can do whichever route they wanted as long as they follow the Guinness rules,' he continued.

'Yesssss!' I remember shouting to myself in my bedroom on hearing of the race. This was it. This was the missing fertiliser that I needed to reignite my love for cycling. The competitive element. Yes, I liked meandering up Britain slowly but what I think I craved was the speed element, the record, the race. If I achieved this, then maybe, hopefully I would become a real big mile cyclist.

Vin's concept of a race around the world was perfect, and happened to coincide nicely with my early mid-life crisis in 2011 and I entered it immediately. 6 months later, on the 18th February 2012, we were all on the start line in Greenwich, London, ready to take on the world. At this point I had somewhat improved as a cyclist and could quite easily cover 200 plus miles a day. This was also the day I was meeting my arch rival, Mike Hall.

Cycling with Vin Cox

There he stood, looking cool, calm and collected. Up until now most us only knew each other via the internet. Now we were actually eyeing each other up, face to face. Mike looked nothing like I had expected. He was about my height, and not in any way very muscular, in fact he seemed to even have a bit of a Yorkshire pudding – a beer belly. As with most ultra and big mile cyclists, a beer after a long ride, and often in the middle, seems to be the standard way to celebrate, not to mention that it's 'calories right' as everyone will admit to saying at least 1,000 times in their cycling career.

Mike wandered over to me pushing his beautiful bike – the black one. He'd gone for full carbon, rims and all, whereas I had gone for a steel bike. Visually my setup looked lighter than his. The steel frame was thinner and I had slightly smaller panniers.

'Hey mate. Are you ready for this?' Mike asked casually as if 'this' was just a little jaunt round the South Downs, not all the way to Australia, and back again.

'I think so. Bloody cold though, can't wait to hit South America.'

'Yeah I saw you're going west, good luck with the headwinds in America mate,' he laughed.

Dammit. He's playing with my mind. I knew it. Yes, I was going to probably face headwinds in America but hated being told so. In my mind I'd magically have tailwinds all the way round the world.

'Can I feel your bike?' he then asked, wanting to see how light it was. Many people had been picking Maid Marion (my bike) up since I arrived at the start and all seemed quite shocked and surprised how light it was.

Myself(left), Mike Hall (2nd from right) and the other Global Bike Race competitors

I knew Mike had seen this, and I knew it was playing on his mind.

'Haha. Not a chance mate,' I laughed back. 'But it's probably lighter than yours,' I winked.

'Fair enough,' he laughed.

'I wouldn't let you pick mine up either.' We both chuckled together.

Truthfully, I knew my setup was probably 2kg heavier than Mike's. I knew this because most of the riders had in the last week given away most of their kit and training details in all their interviews to the cycling media. It was fairly safe to give away your training and kit now being so close to the start. It'd be suicidal for anyone to change their setup a few days before the race. All of us had done thousands of miles on our bikes in training, 10,000 in my case, and we had ironed out everything, the perfect height for your saddle when wearing new bib shorts, and then how much to heighten your saddle when your bib shorts had worn thin after 5,000 miles. These logistics and preparations were just as important as how fit you were. You can be the strongest cyclist in the world but if you get saddle sores and sore knees from unwashed, thinning bibs, you'll never win anything.

And so the countdown began and on 'GO' we all shot down the avenue in Greenwich Park, heading for Australia.

The first month of my ride was incredible. I went through Spain, Morocco, Chile, Peru, Ecuador and then into America. I was averaging about 10 miles per day more than Alan Bates' record and felt strong. I had done just over 4,000 miles in 25 odd days. I remember on day 5 in the American leg (somewhere in Missouri) thinking to myself, 'Well, I think I've only gone and done it. I'm on my way to becoming a real big mile cyclist.'

Sadly just a few days later my dreams came to an end when I was knocked off my bike by a careless driver, suffered a fractured spine, whiplash, concussion, torn ligaments in my ankle, and chipped teeth. My race and my dream of being a real big mile cyclist were over.

After spending nearly a month recovering with the wonderful Missy and Martin Carey who looked after me at their home, I decided not to give up but to carry on, somewhat slower in order to raise money for charity instead. So, after telling my parents that the chances of getting run over twice were practically impossible I set off again with the aid of a local cycling legend, Kurt Searvogel

'Man, I can't believe you cycled on this road man, it's terrible,' Kurt exclaimed when we went back to where I had the accident to continue my ride. It was true. The road was terrible but no worse than I'd cycled in South America. Also, how was I to know? It's just a line on a map at the end of the day. Nowadays you can look at Google street view to gauge the quality of the road but back then you were mostly just winging it.

'Come on. I'll show you some real good Arkansas roads,' Kurt said as we rode off.

I cycled for 2 days with Kurt and he did indeed show me some of the amazing black top roads I should have been cycling on. He was a monster on the bike and would literally cycle circles around me.

'So, you must race?' I asked on catching him up at a set of traffic lights.

'Yeah, but only the long races. 500 miles single staged races you know, and some 24-hour races,' he said

'How do you fetch in them?' I asked.

'Well I usually win,' he said matter of fact. That shut me up. Kurt was a real, no messing around, proper, big mile cyclist, the type that I was so desperately trying to be.

Kurt and I then went our separate ways and I was directed to some better roads west.

While I pedalled along averaging a measly 140 miles per day, Mike was steaming ahead. He was an absolute machine and went on to smash the world record in just under 92 days on the bike, although his official time became 107 days because Guinness, in all their wisdom decided to change to rules for the round the world record soon after he finished. They decided to get rid of the clock stopping rule, which I actually agree with, it was a dumb rule to start with, but to do it soon after Mike had finished was unfair considering they knew all along about the Global Bike Race and were working directly with each rider to validate our routes beforehand. Had we known of this change we would have all taken different routes and had different strategies. It wasn't fair and I felt bad for Mike. Mike, being Mike didn't give two hoots. He was still the fastest in the world and that's all he cared about.

Over a month later I eventually arrived back in London, having only cycled 16,000 miles. Yes, I had cycled very far and when things were going well, very fast too, but it just wasn't meant to be. This time when I cleaned my bike and put it in the shed I had no intention of doing a big bike ride ever again. The passion and confidence were gone. Looking back now I was obviously not in a great frame of mind but at the time I truly believed my cycling adventures were behind me.

Mike never actually filed his record with Guinness, I can only guess because of their stupid rule change so in the following years even more people went on to break Alan Bates' record and claimed the 'official Guinness record'. However, no one got near the actual record Mike had set. That was until 2015 when Lee Fancourt cycled the 18,000 miles in 88 days although he was disqualified for not going back to his position after taking a taxi to help his support crew. Instead of taking the taxi back 50 miles he added 50 miles to the ride which is not allowed. Lee was Marmite to a lot of people and got somewhat alienated by the cycling community due to his often outspoken views, even though his cycling records were incredible. I actually lived near Lee and went out cycling with him. Marmite or not we got along well and there was one thing for sure, he was an astonishing cyclist, and he did it with virtually no money. To watch the pennies he wouldn't do long rides away from home as that would involve having to buy food at service stations, so instead he used to cycle 300 miles on the same 15-mile loop and stop at his house to refuel every 4 or 5 laps. I did a few of these laps with him one day and was bored out of my skull after 6. I bailed and went home and drank some whisky. He did another 10 laps until midnight and passed out on his kitchen floor still in his Lycra.

Getting run over during the Global Bike race

With my cycling adventures behind me I spent the next few years doing other stuff. I became the first person to swim the length of Britain, and then to complete the first ever length of Britain triathlon, I ran it too. It was around this time while I was wasting my life away scrolling through Facebook that I noticed a post. It read:

Tarzan Rides the HAM'R Kurt Searvogel

'Kurt, The HAM'R. No way,' I thought. The HAM'R stands for Highest Annual Mileage Record, better known as The Year Record - Tommy Godwin's record. The machine of a cyclist who had done laps around me in America after my accident was now going for Tommy's record and this was just the beginning of the bigger story that began back in January 2015. This side of the pond there was someone else also having a crack at it – Steve Abraham. Steve started on the 1st January and Kurt on the 10th, a clever tactic by Kurt. The race was on. Although the attempt was the same, Kurt and Steve couldn't have had more polar opposite setups and systems. Kurt had a camper van supporting him throughout the day and he'd drive around chasing the wind and flatlands of Florida. A very good idea. Steve, with a significantly lower budget, was doing long rides from his house in Milton Keynes and carrying a small pannier with things he needed for the day, often stopping at service stations to use the facilities and fill up his water bottles. He passed the time by listening to podcasts about British history, but says he can't remember anything, a sure sign he was pushed to the limit, something the HAM'R does to you.

Kurt was using the latest carbon Time Trial bike and sometimes even a recumbent (a bike that places the rider in reclined position), which I hadn't realised was within the rules but it was. The purist in me wasn't a fan of the recumbent, but cycling is cycling I guess, and if those are the rules then I suppose you got to play the game. Steve was using a steel frame Raleigh. He said he just loved the steel frame and had no issue with using carbon. He would have done so if he'd found a well-fitting one but steel felt more real. He did, however, put an endnote which hinted that he liked that it was a similar setup to Tommy from 1939, and I have to agree – it seemed more authentic and honoured Tommy the way I think he deserved.

Lastly Kurt was doing the record in phenomenally good weather as opposed to Steve who had to deal with the wettest and most miserable times of the year.

The bad weather certainly showed in Steve's earlier mileage and he never once got ahead of Kurt in the first few months. He was hoping, like Tommy had done, that he'd build the bigger miles, 8,000 plus per month when the weather was better.

Three months in, while Kurt was blowing away Tommy's record, Steve was sadly hit by a drunken moped rider and broke his ankle. This is when most of us would have stopped, but not Steve. He continued anyway, knowing full well he had no chance of getting the record. He had time off, started out in a brace on a recumbent trike until he was strong enough to continue on his Raleigh. He had thought of restarting his attempt when he had recovered in August and finished 2015 on 63,606 miles. Nearly 13,000 miles behind Kurt who went on to add 1,000 miles to Tommy's record, covering an astonishing 76,076 miles. It's worth noting Kurt was 53 years old which is even more astonishing. With Steve's restart in August he continued to March 2016 but pulled the plug after realising he was too fatigued after the injury along with cycling solid for 15 months to challenge Kurt's new record.

In the meantime, while Kurt was doing his big rides a young unassuming girl called Amanda Cocker joined him a few times. The HAM'R for women stood at 29,603 miles. Kurt urged Amanda to go for it saying she was certainly strong enough and would smash it. So in May 2016 Amanda started her own Year Record. By July it not only looked like Amanda was going to annihilate the women's HAM'R but she was in fact ahead of Kurt's pace too. She could actually go on to get the overall record too at this pace. The cycling community went into meltdown. Here was a 24-year-old girl destroying the boys and it was awesome. Of course, there were some sceptics, the Tommy Godwin fans, who also didn't like the fact she occasionally used a recumbent too but no one was denying the mental and physical strength was phenomenal. Steve, back home and recovered now, had yet another contestant and restarted his bid in March 2017, for the third time. Steve was months behind Amanda so had a target to chase and was matching her earlier mileage. There was also the possibility that Amanda could still get injured of course, not that he wished it, but that's the game of big mile cycle racing. You never know what might happen to the person ahead of you so you keep on pushing. The leaders take risks to stay ahead and sometimes those risks force them out of the race. Steve never gave up even though he was diagnosed with sleep apnoea and a stomach problem that meant he had to go to the loo 5 times a day, often in a bush on the side of the road.

Amanda not only broke Kurt's Record, she annihilated it with a total distance of 86,573 miles, 11,000 more than Tommy's record.

By September Steve realised he couldn't compete with Amanda but still continued to try and get the male record which was 10,000 miles shorter than the female one. Then in December he got hit by a car again and weeks later slipped on some ice and came down hard on his leg. Being the stubborn cyclist that he was, he continued anyway even though the record was out of reach and ended his year on 72,000 miles, 5,000 miles short of Kurt. Steve had done 166,000 miles between January 2015 and March 2018 and now says he's done with it and has returned to his life delivering pizzas on his bicycle. I do wonder what Steve could have achieved had he had the weather, terrain and often traffic free roads that Kurt and Amanda enjoyed. Sadly I don't think we will ever know but he is only in his early forties, so never say never.

Amanda's year record wasn't the only time a girl has beaten all the boys in a race. The start line of the TransAm, the self-supported bike race across America, hosts all sorts of hardy, tough looking, shaved-legged, lycra clad cyclists, and almost all of them are male. In 2016 this was no different except for one person - Lael Wilcox. Standing out from the crowd, not only for being a girl in a male dominated race, she did not look 'hardy', and did not wear lycra, favouring pink cotton shorts and a grey loose-fitting t-shirt, to the disgust of all the marginal gains, aerodynamics crowd. The only similarity to her male counterparts was the fact that she too had shaved legs.

With virtually no road racing experience she set off with the rest of the bunch and just got on with her own race. As the days passed she soon found herself in 2nd position. No one would believe it. How was a girl in second, beating all the boys? The cycling world was hooked. By the last day with Steffen Stretch in the lead it looked like a girl may actually podium. Sleep deprived Steffen awoke on the last day panicked about being overtaken and made a grave error in navigation - he started cycling back on himself. This is surprisingly easy to do in America when all the main streets look exactly the same and once you've walked around a supermarket a few times and go back outside it's easy for your brain to confuse the time earlier that day, or the day before, when you went into the same supermarket on the other side of the road, so you cycle left instead of right and back on yourself. I nearly did this once in Texas and the only reason I stopped was that all of a sudden I had a headwind when I had a tailwind before. Vin Cox did this and so did Jamie MacDonald when he ran across Canada, running for hours back on himself.

Steffen was going the wrong way. Everyone watching online couldn't believe it, but before one of his friends or family could call him to say; 'Mate, you're going the wrong way,' he came face to face with Lael. I wasn't there but by all accounts, this is something similar to how I imagine their meeting went.

'What, Lael? Are you lost?' asked Steffen.

'No, I think you've gone back on yourself mate,' replied Lael immediately realising the opportunity she was in.

Steffen immediately turned around and pulled alongside Lael. They rode together for a bit and at one-point Lael started going the wrong way and Steffen corrected her back on track.

'Why don't we cycle together to the end? I would have won anyway if I had not got lost. We can cross the line together,' pleaded Steffen who was struggling to keep up. Lael looked over at him and reportedly said.

'This is a race,' and shot off.

Lael sprinted the last 130 miles and Steffen couldn't keep up. Lael won and became the first girl to win the TransAm. The cycling community again came alive and girls all over the world were jumping on their bikes and taking on the boys.

Also in that race was another girl doing well but got somewhat overshadowed. Sarah Hammond came 6th. Sarah, realising she could do better, entered the 2016 Race to the Rock, a 3,000km off road MTB race to Ayers Rock in Australia and in the end was the only person to finish the race. In both 2017 and 2018 she won the race outright.

Back in 2012 during the Global Bike Race there was also a girl in the mix. Her name was Juliana Buhring. She completed the ride in 152 days which when you look at Mike's record seems fairly tame but you must remember that at the time Vin Cox's record had been 163 days. Had Juliana done her ride just 3 months earlier, i.e. before Mike finished, she would have been the fastest person, man or woman, to cycle around the world.

The girls are not only competing alongside the boys in big mile cycling, they are beating them.

With all this new wave of big mile cycling happening all around me it was hard to ignore the urges to get back on the bike. I wasn't quite ready for a cycle only adventure, and certainly not ready for a fastest world record, but after 2 years of swimming and running I decided to do a triathlon, but not any triathlon, the world's longest triathlon and I would do this around the coast of Great Britain.

The swimming and the running part are for a different book entirely but the cycle leg, although not ground breaking by any means, is worth talking about for one reason, and one reason only. I cycled 3,000 miles on a bike made out of bamboo. She was called Matilda and she was absolutely beautiful.

I started the cycle leg from Lulworth Cove in Dorset and immediately realised I had misjudged the steepness and frequency of the hills along the south coast. My days were short, 70 to 100 miles at the most, and on one of the hillier days I had an average cadence of 35. Matilda sadly had some issues. I could only have one ring on the front as there wasn't a clamp big enough for a front derailleur to fit the larger bamboo frame. The chain stays were also at too much of an angle so I had to get rid of the 2 outer gears on the rear cassette. This meant I only had 9 gears to work with and stupidly I chose road gears and not MTB which is what I should have chosen, and my knees were taking the brunt of my lack of planning.

This wasn't the biggest issue however. The main one was than my front wheel was about 10cm off to the right of the frame. It was so bad that whenever I arrogantly passed motorists in a queue for traffic lights and pushed my way to the front, the driver in the car behind me would shout out of their window that my bike was

At John O'Groats for the second time (by bike) during
the cycle leg for my round Britain triathlon

Matilda's wonky frame

Broken and I should stop cycling immediately. My saddle stem was about 2cm off to my left too. The whole bike was a mess and cornering was hazardous to say the least.

Wonky bike and dodgy knees aside, the ride was spectacular. I passed Land's End and worked my way up the coast and eventually reached my second home, John O'Groats. The first time I cycled the length of Britain it took me 25 days. This time, 24 days. Not a great improvement but an improvement none the less. At this rate I'd have a chance at Michael Broadwith's record when I am 107 years old. I joke of course, my coastal route was nearly twice the distance. But even so my daily mileage was dismal. That didn't matter though. This ride wasn't about big miles. It was hopefully going to reignite the fire in my belly for cycling, and that's exactly what it did. I returned home and decided straight away that I needed to enter a proper bike race. I messaged Lee Fancourt to see if he wanted to go for a training ride.

'Of course buddy. Laps tomorrow?' he said and I cringed. I hated to admit it but doing the 15-mile lap over and over and over again was probably good for mind training. If you can survive that, you can survive anything.

I met Lee in a small new build in Gloucester. He was house-sitting for a friend. We went out and hit the road hard. Lee, being a bit heavier than me was thankfully slower on the hills, but once on the flats, down in aero position, I was struggling for dear life to stay on his wheel, ignoring all his elbow flicks to tell me to take the front. Every now and then we'd do a slower lap and ride side by side and chat all things cycling. For Lee his biggest struggle seemed to be sponsorship.

Doing laps with Lee Fancourt

He had been loaned a few bikes in the past and then had to give them back and couldn't afford to buy another bike so inbetween sponsorship deals he would cycle a real pile of crap, but he never managed to make a proper go of it. I have enjoyed wonderful relationships with all sorts of kind-hearted and generous people and companies who've taken a punt on me in the past, and helped me achieve my dreams. Remember I had all but £1 to my name at the age of 30 so I couldn't have done anything without this help. I felt for Lee and wanted to help him. He was a phenomenal cyclist and deserved to realise his huge ambitions. I feared his troubled nature hindered this in some way. People can sense that sort of thing.

'I just aint happy when I'm not riding,' he would say, and I believed it.

After our ride we drank tea, cleaned our bikes and I gave him as much advice as I could about how to get some funding and support for his big rides. I left feeling happy that I had hopefully helped him.

A month later I was in Chicago for the start of the 2016 Route 66 bike race. The countdown began.

'10,9,8 . . .'

My heart started to race. This was it. Route 66 was on and the 30 odd racers were all lakeside at 5am in the morning drizzle.

'3,2,1, Go!'

Everyone shot off, but not at race pace because for the first 15 miles out of town everyone had to stay together. Apparently downtown Chicago isn't a safe place to be cycling alone at 5am and the words *gangland, murdered* and *gunpoint* were mentioned more than enough times to make me believe it.

About 3 miles in, near the back of the peloton, I hit a huge pothole and my water bottle fell out and went sliding across the road. I stopped, turned around and went back for it. By the time I had picked it up the peloton was gone. I was alone. Apart from the panic that I may be murdered, I was also now right at the back of the race, not the place I wanted to be at all.

Throughout the day I picked off riders one by one until around 2pm my phone stopped taking charge from my dynamo – the charge socket had got completely wet from the torrential rain we'd had all morning. This was bad news; I needed to get it fixed. Route 66 was a marked course and any deviation from the set route would mean disqualification and my phone was the only way I could navigate. I lost nearly 2 hours as I faffed around and lost almost all the places I had made. I spent most of the time trying to dry the phone inside a café and in the end just bought a bag of rice which I dunked the bottom of the phone in and decided to carry on cycling. Luckily at this point my friend Jason Woodhouse, who was also in the Global Bike Race of 2012 with me, but didn't finish, cycled past.

'Mate, my phone is bust. Can I follow you while it dries?' I begged.

'Sure buddy. You not using a Garmin?' he asked.

'No, trying to limit the number of things I need to charge,' I replied. A strategy that could save me time but in this case was costing me it.

Jason and I cycled together for a bit and miraculously my phone started charging again and like the gentleman

I was, I dropped him like afterschool voluntary French class and shouted 'Allez, Allez!' for my own amusement.

Slowly I overtook one cyclist after another and eventually I was in third position behind Jay Petervary and Jesse Stauffer. I stayed there for a while and then stopped chasing them as I knew at some point they would sleep, and I would then sleep too. I was pretty much a nobody in this race but I knew I had a chance. I didn't want to give away my trump card just yet, thus making them up their game. Both Jesse and Jay had far more race experience than I did.

By 5am, 24 hours in and having cycled somewhere in the region of 350 miles, a car came up alongside me.

'Hey Barday, fancy a coffee?' The man shouted holding up a large Starbucks.

'I'm just about to head back to give Jesse one too, so all is fair,' he continued.

I feel I should mention why he called me Barday in case some of you search the Route 66 Bike race of 2016 and don't see my name. That's because I changed it for that race. I gave myself a new name. Barday Jeanjé, (a play on the words Beard Ginger) because, well, I had just had a TV show aired on Discovery Channel about the world's longest triathlon and truthfully, I was tired of everyone wanting to know 'What's next?'. My relationship with big mile cycling was fragile at best so I decided to go off and do this race as a different person so that I could just ride, ride for myself, without having people wanting to know all about it. I know it sounds silly but at the time I just wanted a bit of anonymity after months of having cameras in my face.

'No thanks mate. I'm OK. But heading *back* for Jesse? Am I ahead of him?' I asked excitedly as this meant I was now in second position.

'Yes, he just stopped for some food back there.'

'What about Jay?'

'He's sleeping way back,' the guy replied.

I hadn't logged onto the tracking map in a couple of hours. I hadn't expected Jay to sleep so early on.

'So am I in the lead?' I asked.

'I believe so.'

'Cool,' is all I could think to say.

The man veered off and I logged onto the tracking map just to make sure he was telling the truth. Lo and behold I was in the lead. Jay was napping about 10 miles back and Jesse was less than a mile behind me. I figured it'd be nice to have company so I slowed down and Jesse caught me.

'Hey Barday. I'm Jesse,' he said as he came alongside me.

'Actually, my name is Sean.' I explained my name change.

We cycled for 3 hours together and chatted about the various races he had done, most notably he was one of the characters in the film *Inspired to Ride*, where Mike Hall was up against Jason Lane, another pretty impressive big mile cyclist. It was a thrilling race and Mike eventually won. Jesse was cycling with Juliana Buhring, and they both came in tied 4th.

It was great to have some company after feeling guilty for dropping Jason and we sent Mike a message saying we were both leading the race and how we wished he was there. Mike, watching the tracker online would of course have had no idea Barday Jeanje was actually me.

The idea (and we both agreed), was to have a leisurely morning and wait for Jay to catch us. He eventually did and Jesse proceeded to drop me like I dropped Jason, and disappeared off into the sunrise.

'Allez, Allez!' I said softly after them as they rounded the corner and out of sight. Feeling slightly annoyed but deserved because of Karma I decided to have a 45-minute nap to recharge, so found a bush and passed out within seconds. I awoke feeling like a new man. Totally rejuvenated, I carried on in third place.

By midnight that evening I managed to catch both Jesse and Jay who had decided to sleep right near each other but instead of passing them I too found a bush and had another 45-minute nap. Sadly, this time I felt awful when I awoke. My body ached, my eyes struggled to stay open, my head was pounding and my arms and legs felt like they had 50kg weights strapped to each of them. I've never felt so heavy in my life. My pace dropped but I managed to keep in third position for the rest of the day, desperate for a long sleep. That evening I eventually succumbed and had 3 hours tucked under a bush behind a car garage.

The Route 66 bike race of 2016

It was the morning of day 3 when things started to go properly wrong for me. I hit a pothole and came down hard on the saddle. I had one of those 2 prong saddles with 2 front noses and had bruised both sides of my undercarriage. I rushed into a bike shop and bought a normal saddle, hoping when I sat it'd put pressure between my bruises. It didn't work.

With severe pain in my man parts I began holding myself up on the saddle with my quads and eventually at mile 800 or so, with the hills of Missouri taking their toll, I felt it go. The small tendon that joins my quad to my knee had pulled. I tried to carry on for a few more days but eventually realised it was too bad so scratched from the race and limped to Amarillo Airport and flew home, defeated again.

It took 4 days to eventually get back to my boat in Worcester and on the last train from Birmingham I surveyed the landscape. It was flat, like the rest of the Midlands. I ran my thumb over my injured quad tendon and winced when I pressed it, even lightly. I began to wonder if perhaps I would have been stronger had I lived somewhere with hills. Maybe I needed hills in my life to become a real big mile cyclist. What happened next seems extremely unlikely but I can assure you it's exactly as it happened.

I returned to my boat and immediately went online to search for cottages to rent in a hilly part of the UK. I figured 6 months would get me robust enough to become a real big mile cyclist and at the same time I could complete my Running Britain book. It's well documented that authors like mountainous areas to fuel their creativity. There was only one place that I had in mind, The Lake District. Perfect for my hill training and my ambition to be the new Bill Bryson or Wilbur Smith.

This all happened on a Friday and I managed to find a cottage to view near Ullswater. On Monday I drove up, viewed that cottage and 2 others. Signed the papers for one of them on Tuesday, drove back to Worcester, rented a van, packed everything I needed to write and train for 6 months and some furniture. Drove up to the Lakes and back again on the Wednesday, collected my car and by Thursday was all settled into a small 2 bedroom flat just outside Windermere. It was perfect. If I couldn't become a big mile cyclist, or a successful author here, then I couldn't anywhere.

Hill training in the Lake District

After a few months of being settled into my new nest in a woodland outside Windermere, I suddenly thought back to my round the world bike race. The date was the 18th May 2012 and I was in the middle of the outback.

'Crikey mate, are you going for the round Oz record with that lightweight setup. Looks fast,' said an over excited grey-haired chap in his 70's as he pulled up next to me in his campervan. Silver nomads are what they are called I believe. Aussies who retire, sell their home and spend the rest of their years driving around Australia in a campervan.

'No Sir, what record?' I asked not knowing what he was referring to?

'The round Australia cycle record mate. It's like 39 days or something bonkers and the last guy had a set up much like yours.'

'Ah, wow that's fast. No, I'm not going for that record. I'm just cycling around the world at the moment.'

'Ah, fair dinkum mate. Good luck. When you're done with that come back and go for the Oz record mate. I'm sure you'd smash it.'

It was then that the seed was planted, all the way back in 2012.

It was now November 2016 and it had been nearly 5 years since I heard about the Oz record and I was now 36 years old and finally ready for it. My withdrawal from Route 66 hadn't dampened my spirits completely and I was looking for something else to sink my teeth into. Could it be Australia? It was a big ask and I'd need to seriously increase my mileage and speed. At 37 odd days

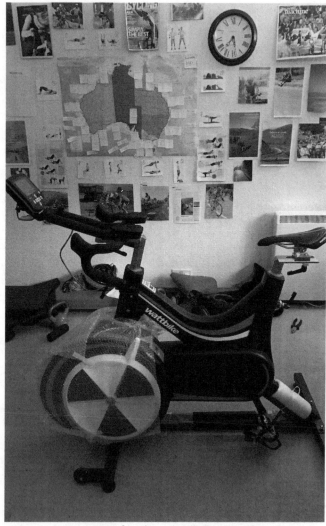

Preparing for the round Oz record

(the record at the time), this would be my shortest challenge to date. I decided to wait till the New Year to decide.

New Year came and went and I was in Northern France with Caroline (my then girlfriend, and now wife) and her family. Waking up to 10 inches of snow was just the motivation I needed to go off and do something in a warm country for a change. It was then I decided to commit. Australia here I come!

There was also a race in Australia called the Indian Pacific Wheel Race that went from Perth to Sydney. It was happening in March and I had been hoping to enter it as a training ride. Mike sent me a message

'You heading to Australia at all?' he wrote.

'That's hopefully the plan. But I'm really fat and unfit. Ha,' I joked. It was true though, I wasn't in my best form.

'Cool. Yeah, I'm not the fittest either but there's a bit of time yet,' he continued.

'You doing TD (Tour Divide) again?' I asked.

'Not this year – to close to the TCR really – gets a bit stressy.'

'Aha. Did you see Guy Martin pulled out of GB (Great Britain) lap?' Guy and Mike cycled together for a while during the Tour Divide and knew they'd stayed in touch since then.

'Yeah he said he was full of cold when he set off. I'm not sure I fancy that one – but need to do a LEJOG at some point.'

'Hahaha. Yes you do.' I replied.

Australia was coming together nicely for me and I couldn't wait to head down under and give the Aussies a seeing to, and show them how it's done, on their home soil.

Sadly I couldn't make it down under due to other work commitments, and most importantly, trying to raise the tens of thousands of pounds in funding for my Lap of Oz, as I would need a full support crew to break the current record. It was an expensive task.

I was really gutted to miss out on the Indipac race because I had been looking forward to being on the start line with Mike even though I wasn't nearly fit enough to compete against him. He was at the top of his game and a main contender for the win even though the competition was really high with a few of the big players in the big mile cycling world in the race too. Sarah Hammond, Kristof Allegaert and Jesse Carlsson, all understated superstars in the world of big mile cycling gunning for a podium spot. I say podium but the end of these races often sees the winner come in alone, usually at 3am because they've done an all-nighter on the last day, with no crowds, no cheers, no podium. Just a celebratory slap on a monument or wherever people have decided the end of the race is. In fact, for insurance purposes, some big mile cycling races aren't even official races, they are technically flash mobs where people all get together and agree to cycle from one place to another. No prize money, no huge media crews, no hype. Just a bunch of people who want to ride their bikes far and fast and Mike was arguably the best in the world. It was going to be one hell of a race.

The day before they all set off I sent Mike a good luck message. I presumed he was getting hundreds of messages so didn't expect a reply.

'Go get 'em mate. Good luck.'

Moments later Mike replied in the understated way he always did.

'Ta.'

Little did I know that would be the last time I would ever hear from him.

31 March 2017
ACT Police

"About 6.25am, police responded to a report of a collision on the Monaro Highway towards Williamsdale between a car and a cyclist."

"ACT Ambulance Service attended and the male cyclist was pronounced deceased at the scene."

"ACT Policing's Collision Investigation and Reconstruction Team (CIRT) are examining the circumstances surrounding the collision."

My heart sank and tears rolled down my face. I was all alone on the other side of the world in a hotel in Cape Town when I heard the news. The man I respected the most in big mile cycling, Mike Hall, had been tragically killed in Australia on the last day of the Indipac race.

In losing a friend, I lost the drive for big mile cycling, especially in Australia. For hours I sat there on the bed sobbing. Mike was one of the most experienced cyclists on the planet, far more than I will ever be.

Although Mike and I weren't by any means tied at the hip, when someone you know dies doing something that you love, it really makes you think about everything. Over the next few months as much as I tried to stay focused on Australia I just couldn't find the motivation to get on my bike. Why had this happened to Mike? What was the point to all this endurance cycling? Were the risks really worth it?

Suddenly my goal to become a big mile cyclist felt hedonistic and selfish. I was torn between the real world of life and death and my ultimate dream of setting an big mile cycling record. If I achieved this I would be ticking the third and final box in my quest for achieving the Three F's – the holy grail in the world of endurance – a world's First, a Fastest and a Furthest. If you manage to get a world record in each of those categories, as three separate, significant, solo events, you practically become endurance royalty. I had successfully completed a world's *First* – Swimming the length of Britain, and a world's *Furthest* - the world's longest triathlon, but the third and final F, a world's *Fastest*, had eluded me for years. Australia was going to be my attempt at a *Fastest*, and before Mike's death I had felt, both physically and mentally, the strongest I'd ever felt in my life. I was very confident that I would achieve my dream of getting that third and final F and finally become a proper, real, bona fide, big mile cyclist.

As the months rolled by it became clear that I was nowhere near able to turn my Australia record dream into a reality. I was way behind my training schedule, lacked any glimpse of that thing called motivation that for years was my biggest asset, and was constantly questioning everything in life, purpose, community, family, risk, the lot. There wasn't a minute in each day where I didn't think about something mind bogglingly philosophical about what I should be doing with my time on this planet, yet I didn't have the brain capacity to think of any of the answers. I really felt like I was wasting my life. Mike famously said; 'You can't take yourself too seriously. It's just riding bicycles at the end of the day.' Was that enough? It seemed enough for him but I was struggling to justify the risks involved.

My uncertainty obviously showed through when I went to meet people and businesses who were thinking about funding the Australian record bid, because no-one was biting and the one big lead I had, pulled out. Eventually with not enough funding in place, the weather window closing, and absolutely no ambition to actually get on my bike, I had to cancel my dream of trying to break the round Australia world record. It was a tough decision as I had already put together an amazing support crew who had taken time off work specially to get involved. Disappointing them was by far the hardest thing. Way more than having to return all the funding that I had received already, even though I had spent some of it in the planning stage. 2017 was not going well at all and I was at my lowest point in a very long time. I just didn't know how to fall back in love with cycling.

Feeling rather depressed by my failures as a cyclist, I caught up with Mark Beaumont in London for a pint. We were both there doing motivational talks for some important well-dressed folk in the city.

'Alright amigo. Looking smart.'

'As are you sir,' I replied. Neither of us wear smart clothing in our normal lives but we do when we give talks. I actually quite like it. Putting on a suit becomes somewhat of an occasion for me. My current 'talk' suit is also the suit I wore for my wedding, which makes me smile.

After Mark's 2008 round the world record, he cycled the Americas for a BBC documentary and then hung up his cycling boots for a while and concentrated on other things. It wasn't until 2015 when he returned to big mile cycling and broke the Cairo to Cape Town cycling record in a time of 41 days, 10 hours, 22 minutes. Now back in the big mile cycling game, it was clear he wanted to do an even bigger ride, something that no one will ever do again.

I could see Mark was buzzing and as always it wasn't long before we ask each other the most frequently asked question of all time:

'So, what's next?'

I explained my lack of enthusiasm for getting on the bike of late and just needed to sort my head out. Mark was in different spirits altogether. I could see it in his eyes.

'Promise this stays between us,' Mark said in a lowered tone, looking around in case someone was listening.

'Lips are sealed mate.'

'It's pretty obvious though. I'm sure you can guess?'

'Australia? Are you going for the Oz record?' My heart sank. It would be just my luck wouldn't it?

'Ha. No but that would have been fun, a race.'

'I know right,' I laughed back, my mood doing a 180 as I began thinking how good an idea that actually would have been. Sean vs Mark. Truthfully, at 85kg Mark would always win a flat course like Oz. I weigh 65kg so would need a hillier challenge.

'Come on, it's obvious. I'm going to do it again,' he said and put his finger in the air drawing some sort of halo above his head.

'You want to become an angel?' I asked sarcastically.

'The world. But this time in 80 days. I think it's possible.'

My mouth dropped open. Around the world in 80 days. It was genius. Nick Sanders had done it in 1984 when the mileage was 13,000. For Mark to do it in 80 days under the new rules of 18,000 miles and no clock stopping meant he'd have to actually do it in 76 odd days with 4 days travel, a whopping 240 miles per day.

As we all now know Mark went on to successfully achieve his dream of cycling around the world in 80 days and completed the ride in 2017 in 78 days, 14 hours and 40 minutes. Physically it was obviously ferociously difficult but what's more impressive for me is the overall logistics of making that ride happen. A team of 40 people, support vehicles, camper vans, scientists, and nutritionists all hard at work making sure Mark's legs, and more importantly his mind, were up to the task. His book about it is well worth a read.

Inspired by Mark and returning home to my half-built Australia bike sitting in the corner I decided the only way to get back on the proverbial horse, was to get back onto the non-proverbial and very real bike. I thrive on goals and moping around my flat wasn't doing me any good.

I scoured the internet for inspiration. I needed some record to beat, some record to become the fastest in, to finally get my third F. Then I came across the Facebook page of German endurance cyclist Jonas Deichmann. His page said that at the beginning of July he was going to attempt 2 world records. One being the fastest to cycle across Europe, and the second to carry on and get the overall Europe and Asia world record too, or the Eurasia World Record as it's called.

By now I've come to know exactly when I love an idea, my heart rate goes up, my imagination runs wild, and I immediately have the urge to buy a large map. I wasn't interested in the full Eurasia record however, I could follow shortly after him, kind of like racing him, chasing him, and take the Europe world record off him. He would still, of course, get his record; I would just take it off him, like he would be taking it off the chap before him. Maybe this could be my third and final F – the fastest crossing of Europe by bicycle. I went online immediately and bought the biggest map of Europe I could find. It arrived the next day and I stuck it on the wall with blue tack. I then placed my Wattbike right in front of it and jumped on. I slowly spun my legs and examined it in all its glory. Portugal to a part of Russia that's in line with Afghanistan. Or, in other words, not far off the distance from the UK to the Chinese border. It would be 4,000 miles, a better distance for me. Route 66 I think had been too short at 2,000 miles. It meant I'd be cycling for about 3 weeks which would give me time to get into the swing of things. I found that I only got good after 10 days to 2 weeks. Europe was the perfect distance for me but I'd still need to work on my speed.

'I must text Lee,' I thought. He'd be great to train with because he has a similar world record to his name. Lee has the length of Europe (Tarifa in Spain to North Cape in Norway) record. It's a little over 4,000 miles, so of similar distance. I thought how cool it would be if he has the north/south record and I got the west/east record. I also wanted to see how he was doing with sponsorship and everything else. It had been a while since we spoke.

I didn't text Lee that day as it slipped my mind.

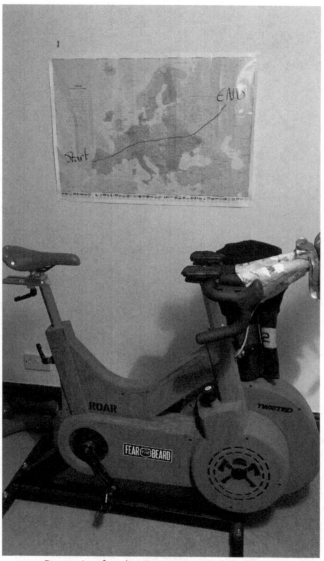

Preparing for the Europe record in 2017

Cabo Da Roca 2017

Europe was on. The definition according to Guinness who adjudicate these records, said that Europe (in their books anyway), was from the most westerly point of Portugal all the way across to a town in Russia called Ufa, which was in line with Afghanistan. You could take any route as long as you cycled every single one of the 4,000 odd miles. I did find a route which was around 3,900 miles but it included more hills in the Alps which I was trying to skirt around. There is some formula that states for every 1,000 metres of climbing it's still quicker to do an extra 30 flat miles. This made planning a wider route to detour the alps a mathematical nightmare. Luckily my inability to be bothered with that level of planning meant I was just going to wing it. Someone famously said 'with the right amount of planning you can successfully eradicate all adventure out of your adventure'. I fully support that theory. Adventure is not all about rowing oceans or climbing mountains. Adventure in its purest form is simply a way of thinking. All that said, there was obviously a certain level of planning that I needed to do, otherwise the record would be out of my reach. I looked at my diary and departing on the 5th of August 2017 was my best option. Butterflies were slowly awakening in my stomach. I had missed that feeling.

Seeing as I already had my Australia bike and some level of fitness, I spent the next few months getting in as much training as possible and trying to work around other commitments. At this time of year these were mainly giving key-note talks to companies and prize-giving lectures to schools, talking about the importance of resilience, keeping a level head, team-work, building a strong foundation and aiming high. So between driving 10,000 miles a month doing talks to raise the funding, and the constant rain in The Lake District, it was a struggle to get all the miles in the legs that I needed, but was still confident that the Europe record was within reach.

September eventually came around and I flew out to Portugal with Caroline for a week's holiday before the record. She brought her bike too and it was exactly what I needed. Gentle day rides, relaxing, reading books and mentally preparing for the record. I don't think I've felt so relaxed or prepared for anything. All my ducks were in a perfect row, silently waiting to be unleashed, ready to morph into raging bulls.

Cabo da Roca was exactly how I expected it. Loads of tour buses of people all there for nothing other than to say they've been to the most westerly part of mainland Europe. A bit like the people who go to Land's End or John O'Groats. It was at least a bit sunnier in Portugal.

10am was to be my start time which would allow Caroline to cycle with me for the first few hours back towards Lisbon where she would leave me and fly home.

9.59am

10,9,8 . . . we counted down together.

3,2,1, Go. Go. Go.

We cycled off up the hill and back through the forests towards Lisbon. It was tough to say our goodbyes at a random, impersonal train station but I promised that I'd be safe and reminded her that no-one gets run over twice in life, and I've had my turn. We kissed each other goodbye and I disappeared up the busy road.

For the next few days I blasted my way across Portugal and Spain and was way ahead of Jonas and feeling as confident as ever when things started to go wrong. The injury gods were back. I seemed to have pulled my quad muscle, the same as I had done on Route 66. I continued for a further few days but it soon became clear I just couldn't push much more than 150 miles per day, well short of my daily target and it seemed the injury was getting worse. It was clear I could not carry on. I sat down on the side of the road somewhere near Pamplona, my head spinning. Maybe trying to get that third and final F, and a cycling world record, was just not in the stars for me. A few hours later I decided to pull the plug and turned left and cycled into Pamplona where I checked into a hotel and slept for 2 days.

2017 had not been a good year for me and I very nearly gave it all up but Europe was still niggling me. I knew I could do it. I just knew it. Something in my gut kept saying.

'Have another go my son. Come on. You know you want to.'

The mileage was tough but not impossible. I could have a few bad days and still break the record, and most of all, it would be one hell of an adventure. As with many of these records a couple of people each year have a crack at them and I knew that a certain Leigh Timmis, a touring cyclist who spent 7 years cycling around the world was due to do a fully supported ride across Europe in July. As Guinness don't differentiate between supported vs unsupported, and I wasn't interested in doing Europe supported, I'd have to get in before Leigh if I was to have a chance. Once someone goes fully supported the only way to break their record is to go supported yourself. Supported rides really are that much faster. There is no excuse to do less than 200 miles a day on supported rides where you have nutritionists, masseuses, doctors and drivers all helping you do nothing except cycle. If I were to give it a go I needed to commit soon, otherwise I'd not have the time to get fit enough.

A few weeks later I got a message from Jason Woodhouse.

'Have you heard about Lee? So sad.' He sent a link to a post on Facebook. I opened it.

'Oh boy, I have some sad news.

Some of you will know we supported the Gloucester cyclist, Lee Fancourt on his many crazy world record rides around the UK and even the world.

I'm afraid Lee was found unconscious today and later passed away, having taken his own life . . .'

I stopped reading. My heart sank and all I could think about was that text I was meant to send, but didn't. Maybe I could have helped, somehow, with something, anything. Lee was such a strong cyclist but battled with his own mind and in the end, his mind won and cycling lost. It was tragic beyond words.

I decided there and then to have another crack at Europe and I would do it, silently, in honour of Mike and Lee. Life was just too bloody short not to grab every opportunity possible.

I had just 4 months to get fit. Winter was tough. It snowed all the way until April 2018 which made training on the indoor trainer all the more tiresome. It's difficult to explain just how tedious it is to retrain for something that you've previously failed at. Anyone who's ever decided on a big challenge will know that some of the most exciting bits are buying a map, unrolling it on your kitchen table, that fresh smell of new paper stimulating all your senses as you nervously look at all the new places you're going to explore. That nervous excitement then fuels you to get on your bike immediately and ride all day and night before coming home, collapsing in a heap on the kitchen floor because that's the only floor in your house that isn't carpeted, and you don't want to leave a salty sweat stain on your carpet. You feel exhausted, nauseous, shivering and you love it. The months of planning, logistics, hours of scouring eBay for bargain bits of kit you need, and scrolling through hundreds of miles of Google street view to check for road quality and size of hard shoulder, all add to the adventure.

This I had already done the previous year. The map was already on the wall, I had all the kit and I had even placed a sweat mat down in the dining room as a better alternative to the hard kitchen floor to fall onto when exhausted beyond measure. There was now nothing to get me excited. Nothing at all except the unrelenting task of trying to get miles in the legs, and even that was a tough slog over winter.

With just over a month before my departure, I decided to cycle to Liverpool and catch the ferry to Belfast and cycle as much around Ireland as I could in a few weeks. I overloaded my bike to add weight and set off in the pouring rain and spent 2 weeks cycling in and out of every cove and back road around Northern Ireland, and then down into Ireland. It's amazing how quickly fitness returns and I ended the ride with a nice little 140-mile coast to coast – Galway to Dublin in under 10 hours including 2 stops for pizza. I was ready for Europe part 2 and nothing suggested any injury to my right leg. Finally, I felt strong enough.

Eventually departure day arrived and I said rushed, tearful goodbyes to Caroline at Manchester Airport and flew back out to Portugal for the second time. This was it. I had one last go at trying to get this Europe record. I could feel the weight of the last 10 years bearing down on my shoulders. Part of me felt confident but no matter how much I tried to ignore it, there was still the glaring fact that not one of my cycling records attempts had gone to plan. I had failed, a lot, and it was hard to ignore the possibility of failure again. But this time I feared the failure would be the last straw. I feared that if I failed again, I would give up cycling altogether and that would be just so very sad.

Back at Cabo da Roca, Portugal

PART TWO — THE RACE

Race Time: 0 Days. 0 Hours. 0 Minutes
Location: Cabo da Roca, Portugal
Miles Cycled: 0

'I'm a genius,' I said to myself smugly. Depart at 5pm on day 0, cycle all through the night and all through the next day and then sleep at around 11pm on night 2. That would mean a good 30-hour session on the bike which would hopefully bank me some good miles and bring my daily average down a notch going forward. The extra bonus was that by starting at 5pm on day 0 meant my target for Ufa, Russia was midnight on the 11th May, a nice round easy time to remember. Truthfully, it was actually 34 minutes past midnight so I had that extra half an hour on top, just in case. I know it sounds silly that you'd need an easy time to finish in order to get the record, however you'd be surprised how much energy you use with simple tasks like working out your finishing time. Random times like 3.54am adds far too much maths in moments of fatigue. Midnight was far easier to remember.

I emailed my map guy, Anthony Goddard, who lives in America and asked him to turn my tracker on at 5pm Portugal time. The plan was set and I snuggled in for a good 15 hours sleep.

What I hadn't quite appreciated was that in order for this to actually work, for me to be able to cycle for 30 hours straight, which I have done many times before, I'd have really needed to sleep until 4pm in the afternoon, which obviously I didn't. In fact I awoke at the ridiculous time of 5.39am to the sound of 2 yapping little dogs from the house next to the B&B and didn't fall back asleep again. I should have started cycling right then but Anthony was still fast asleep in America and couldn't turn the tracker on. I decided to just stick to my original plan so got up to build Miss Moneypenny, the name the internet had suggested for my bike.

I piled everything on the floor and went through each item again giving them intense scrutiny as to their importance on this ride.

The list was as follows:

Stanforth Conway Bike - Reynolds 853 steel frame.
Reynold aero 46 wheels
SP dynamo hub
Supernova dynamo light

B&M charge regulator
Continental GP4000's tyres x3 (2 on the bike. 1 spare)
TT bars
Bar end mirrors
Rear bike lights x6
Cycle computer
Quad-lock phone mount
Road pedals
Brooks Cambium C13 saddle
Restrap panniers
1 litre water bottles x2
Limar helmet
Helmet front and rear light
Sunglasses
Quoc road shoes
Gloves x2 (summer and winter)
Leggings
Buff
Down gilet
Bib shorts
Long sleeve jersey
Long sleeve waterproof
Socks x1 pair
Tennis ball called Wilson
Little Flying Cow mascot
Small knife
Chain oil
Headphones
SPOT tracker
iPhone cables x5
Micro-USB cables x3
Bremont watch
Fake wallet (to give muggers)

Real wallet (which I hide in shorts)
Freeloaded Sixer solar battery bank
GoPro
Letters from Caroline to read every 1,000 miles
Language cards
Pump
Spare inner tubes x2
Bike tool
Sun cream
Cable ties
Elastic bands x6
Superglue
Self-stick puncture repair patches x20
Traditional puncture repair kit
Toilet paper
Tyre removal tools x4
AAA batteries
Spare chain quick links x5
Tera-Nova Bivvy
Therm-a-rest Neo-Air camping mat
Haglofs down sleeping bag
Blow up camping pillow
Half a toothbrush
Spork
Phone

Total weight. 15.5kg

All the kit for cycling across Europe

By lunchtime everything was in its rightful place, toothbrush and spork cut in half and velcroed to the aero bars along with some hay fever and Imodium tablets and a permanent marker to write things on my arm that I needed to remember, like cycle faster, or drink more water. Whatever I felt I was forgetting I would write on my arm. I also had a laminated note tied between the aero bars facing me. It read:

Eat Every Hour
Drink Bottle Every 2 Hours
***** SALT ******
Remember Why
Smile and Stretch
Peanut Butter, Crisps, Banana
Fruit, Veg, Chorizo, Milkshake

These were the things that I deemed most important in order for me to break the record and the most important of the lot was 'Remember Why.' For Mike and Lee.

I then spent 5 minutes putting my various rear bike lights on the frame. I had 6 in total. This along with some reflective tape on the stays and a cut up fluorescent builders' jacket on the rear pannier made me the most visible I could possibly have been. I got the rear lights from my friend Rory from Upgrade Bikes. He sent me a bunch of Lezyne lights with a note saying.

'No one wants to run over a cyclist. Make it as easy as possible for them not to.'

I had never really thought about it in that way before. With the seemingly standard nearly war-like 'Cyclist vs Cars' headlines that get thrown around, it's difficult not to think that all cars want to run you over at every given chance, but the reality is that no-one wants to at all. Many drivers nowadays are in fact cyclists too. This thought actually made me feel a lot better and I knew whenever I had a close shave in Russia, I'd keep thinking about it.

A few hours later I had done the 2-hour cycle and was back at the start line – Cabo da Roca. It was strange being back. The same familiarity, the same tour buses, the same sea breeze. This time, however, it was even busier. Hundreds of people wandered around taking photos of the lighthouse and surrounding landscapes all on their own adventures, only occasionally giving me a second glance which I tend to always get anywhere in the world due to my now ridiculously large beard. I sat there in the sunshine awaiting my 5pm start. With each minute I got more and more nervous. I just wanted to start there and then but knew I couldn't.

Not only was my ride being tracked, Anthony had taken the tracking data from Jonas' ride the previous year and created a ghost figure that would leave at the same time as me. In essence I was actually racing him. We were going head to head and although he wouldn't actually be there (obviously), it felt like a good old-fashioned bike race. Jonas would get to Ufa at midnight on the 11th May too (well, 34 minutes past midnight) and as long as I was ahead of him, I was still in the lead. The one difference being, I was starting at 5pm and I think Jonas started at 8am or something so we'd be on different clocks. So it's likely he'd overtake me when I slept and vice versa. It would no doubt be all very exciting, both for me, and for my friends and family following the tracker back home.

Eventually it was 4.53pm and I slowly meandered through the crowds down to the start. There were hundreds of people, most with selfie-sticks, taking and retaking the same photo to get it perfect for Instagram. I hated it and again wished I had started in the early morning when no one was around. I just wanted to get going and let real life disappear for the next 3 weeks.

As much as I hated being in the mob of Instagram tourists I needed to concentrate on the task at hand. I desperately needed to hit the ground running. I could lose this record if I had one disastrous day but equally could win it if I played these first 30 hours well.

'Build a lead, Sean. Never have to chase,' I kept repeating to myself.

4.59pm

The countdown was on, again. Anthony had messaged me saying he was ready to hit the play button and for the record to officially begin.

10,9,8,7. I counted down. The familiar racing of my heart clouded out all other noises.

3,2,1 . . . Go! I said to myself and 3 people who had seen my attempt on Facebook all cheered and waved me off. For the next 25 days I'd be sitting on a piece of rubber smaller than my hand. Let's hope my backside would hold out.

The hilly forested national park of Sintra made way for bustling suburban Lisbon, busy roads, hooting cars and miles and miles of traffic lights and roundabouts. Luckily I knew the route. In fact I'd know the route all the way to the Pyrenees and I was going to use this to my advantage. Unlike last time the wind gods were looking favourably on me and I had a stonking tailwind. So much so I decided to forfeit my first lunch stop and had an energy bar instead. I was averaging 16 miles per hour and that included the traffic lights and a short break to get a banana and refill my water bottles while adding my special mix to it — salt and chia seeds. Scooping one spoonful using my sawn-in-half-to-save-weight spork gave me satisfaction that I've yet to experience elsewhere. The mind is a powerful thing.

The salt thing came from when, years previously, I had the opportunity to be tested in the GSK laboratories in London. They have state of the art equipment and technology that tests for everything, blood sugar, VO2, max power, lactate threshold, cognitive function, sweat loss and salt loss. I also had the misfortune of going in for testing after both Chris Froome and the Brownlee brothers and I can tell you one thing. If you ever feel like you're at the top of your game physically, compare your stats to that of a professional. It's safe to say I was quite significantly more rubbish than all three of those men. Other than the disappointment of realising I'm not a magnificent genetic freak of nature that'll be written about in biology exams for centuries, (something everyone who gets tested secretly hopes for) I did learn I lose 3.4g of salt in every litre of sweat and I sweat a litre an hour in 30 degrees. Most people only lose 1g to 1.5g of salt per hour. This means if I go all day in the heat I'd need upwards of 40g of salt per day. The UK recommended allowance is 6g per day so that is why I made my special salt and chia mix. The chia truthfully does pretty much nothing for me in such small volumes, however I still feel the psychological benefits knowing full well it's all placebo effect. As I said, the mind is a powerful thing. Oh, and on a side note, I'm also two hundredths of a second slower than Jensen Button at my reaction speeds. That is quite a lot if you're a racing car driver. So it's a good thing I'm just a completely average cyclist then.

It wasn't until around 11pm when I first started to doze off on the bike. It came as quite a surprise when this happened and wasn't what I was planning. I knew I was tired but not this tired. As anyone who's planned a big challenge will know, the lead up is always chaotic and often once you start, your body finally decides: 'Right, all the hard work is over mate, time to relax now.'

This is exactly the opposite of what you actually need, you know, fight or flight and all that. Now should be the time when it's all guns blazing, marauding a trail across the Portuguese landscape. Nevertheless, I was tired, beyond tired. Lack of sleep, long flights and a busy lead up now left me with nothing in the tank. And then at the stroke of midnight, as if almost a sign that if I carried on I would fall asleep on the bike, I got a flat tyre. That was my cue to have a nap. I went off no more than 3 metres from the side of the road and lay down. The intention was to have 3 hours sleep, more than enough to get over my drowsiness I hoped.

The cockpit

Race Time: 0 Days. 9 Hours. 45 Minutes
Location: Tancos, Portugal
Miles Cycled: 100

I never managed anywhere near 3 hours but I must have had about an hour's sleep and got up at 2.45am, replaced my inner tube and carried on.

As the sun rose through the mist, and droplets of water soaked my beard, life seemed much slower than it had done yesterday. I finally got to think about what lay ahead of me. 4,000 miles, 8 or 9 countries, (depending if I went into Switzerland or not), 250-300 litres of water to be drunk, and about 200,000 calories to be eaten, which is 394 Big Macs or 870 Mars Bars. Sleep would be a comfortable 4-6 hours a night which is, believe it or not, quite a luxury for a race of this distance. Not only was I constantly working out how much food, water, salt and sleep I needed each day, I also needed to make sure I was staying ahead of Jonas. It's easy to fall into the 'well I'll do a few short days to start and do the bigger days once I'm into the swing of things'. That never works. It means you're constantly chasing your tail and often make bad decisions in haste. Don't push too hard at the start either. You'll never recover. Best to keep a good steady average in line with the record, and when the patented *Sean Conway Five Pistons of Endurance* are all working, then attack.

People have often asked me what makes a big mile cyclist go further and faster and it's the 5 following things. Food, Water, Sleep, Muscle Management, and most importantly, Mindset. Get all these working well, then you'll do good mileage. It sounds simple, but I can assure you it's very difficult when you're self-supported. One of these things will always be sub-par and in turn will throw everything off kilter – just like a misfiring engine. You can have had the best sleep in the world, feel refreshed, eaten loads but if you are even the slightest bit dehydrated, you just won't push big miles. Or you can have good food, water, mind-set and muscles, but if you sleep too much, you will be behind schedule. It's a fine art to get the right balance of each element, and to try and do it while fatigued, cold, wet and miserable. The people who do this successfully, are the people who win races. I was not one of those people, yet.

Today for me was the real start of the race. I decided to ignore the first 7 hours where I'd cycled 100 miles and considered them bank miles, or bonus miles. I now had

25 full days, midnight to midnight, to complete the 4,000 odd miles, or thereabouts, depending how lost I got. The race was now officially on. There was however a second mileage reference each day. That was how many miles I had done by 5pm. This only really made any sense for the first few days, more for interest than anything else. This would be my actual 24-hour ride distance from the start – 5pm to 5pm. For some reason, and writing this I can't even begin to know why I gave it so much importance, but this seemed to be the figure that I focused on. It shouldn't have been and I wasted countless energy on the maths surrounding it when in fact the midnight to midnight from the start of day 2 was a far better target to aim for. But nevertheless I wanted to see what I was actually achieving in the first 24, 48 and 72 hours so spent most of the day trying to guess my average pace and what my resulting mileage may become by 5pm. I should have been thinking about everything on my laminated notes instead, and in turn, I struggled along all morning with maybe only 2 of my 5 pistons firing, muscle management and mindset. Food, water and sleep all far below where I needed them to be, and it was a lot hotter and a lot harder to find well-stocked service stations in Portugal than I remembered. My average pace was right down at 10mph, including stops.

The midday heat rose into the 30's Celsius which was hot but not as unbearable as it had been the year before where I had to dose myself with any water I could find: town fountains, streams, the car water tap at service stations, overpriced bottles of sparkling water (because they had run out of still water), anything to cool myself down.

Feeling sluggish and weak all day, it came as somewhat of a surprise that by 5pm I had cycled 222 miles. A fairly good 24 hours but a slow day in actual terms as I was only 122 miles in and that had taken me 14 hours. I was just so very fatigued, fatigued from the lead-up, life admin back home, over-training and under-eating, a fatigue that takes weeks to recover from, a fatigue that I never got over for the remainder of the ride across Europe, but at the time I didn't know it, and thankfully so.

By nightfall and after a terrible day on the bike covering only 130 miles, I decided to find a bush and have a proper sleep. I had pushed it too hard on the first day and was paying for it now. Get a good sleep and carry on tomorrow. I was, by the looks of things, about 60 miles ahead of Jonas. With any luck when I awoke he wouldn't have overtaken me.

Constantly doing maths

Race Time: 1 Day. 12 Hours. 0 Minutes
Location: Sabugal, Portugal
Miles Cycled: 230

I set my alarm for 5am. Quite a lie-in considering. I immediately logged onto the tracking map to see where Jonas was. Good news. He wasn't near me. I started to scroll back on the route but couldn't see him. I scrolled forward but couldn't see him either. I then zoomed out and my heart sank. He was not only ahead of me, but miles ahead. I couldn't quite believe it. How had he managed such a big day?

Within 8 minutes I was up and back on Miss Moneypenny, brushing my teeth in the dark as I cycled along.

By 6am I climbed all the way up to the Spanish border. It was cold, worryingly cold and I wore every bit of clothing I had brought. My hands especially were freezing. This wasn't a good sign because Ufa was currently still in negative degrees Celsius. I only hoped that by the time I got there, it would have warmed up a bit. This I feared may have been a huge miscalculation.

Over the top and then the long downhill into Spain the cold cut me in half. I hunched over the handlebars, shoulders up, groaning incessantly, resembling something not dissimilar to the Hunchback of Notre Dame. This thought at least made me giggle as I fell into full character and groaned and growled at every cow I passed until the first rays of light warmed me up just enough to lose interest in cycle-based pantomime. How childish it all suddenly seemed in this very serious endeavour.

The cold aside, Spanish roads are a joy to cycle on. Wide hard shoulders and aside from town centres, I found the drivers to be pretty respectful. I wistfully watched the sun rise again for the second time and took comfort in the thought that I'd get to see the sun rise and set every single day for 25 days, something I admittedly don't do very much during the summer months.

Service stations in Spain seemed far better stocked than in Portugal which meant food and water were no issue. I had had a good sleep and my mood was high. If only my legs weren't so stiff then I'd be firing on all cylinders. Maybe tomorrow will be the day to attack, not today. Still, road conditions were good enough for me to hopefully do around 180 miles. I needn't do any more than that really.

My third breakfast consisted of 3 packets of chorizo sticks, 2 bags of crisps, 1 litre of strawberry milkshake and a banana. Stops limited to 14 minutes I was soon back in tri position, elbows down on aero bars playing a game I invented when I cycled around the world – White Line Chicken. The idea was to see how long you can cycle along the white line without looking ahead. I'd first scour the road for any rocks or potholes in my way and if none I'd put my face almost on the handlebars and focus on keeping my wheel within the white line. This takes surprisingly more courage than you'd expect and usually within 10 metres or so I'm envisaging a rampaging bull running out into the road in front of me, or a snake . . . dammit, a snake. I jump back onto my grips and swerved off the road. I looked back to see a one metre long snake slither across the road and back into the grass, none the wiser that he, or she (it's hard to tell with snakes), nearly lost a tail; White Line Chicken 1 – Sean 0.

Salamaca came and went and I took with it half a pizza wrapped in a plastic bag and stuffed into my jersey back pocket for later in the day. For the first time in the ride I was actually taking in the scenery, looking left and right and even greeting people as I passed them by. The Mindset piston happily firing away pushing me forward.

It was around 3pm when I suddenly spotted it. Bleached white on the side of the road, covered in bits of lichen. It was a very old skeleton and not that of a sheep as is most common in my world living in the Lake District. This was a ferocious animal, its top jaw showing large canine teeth. I stopped and turned back to inspect it. The skeleton was that of a large dog. It was strangely beautiful lying there in the long grass and by the looks of things had been there possibly a decade judging by the decay, although I'm no expert. I suddenly felt sad for it, lying there alone with nothing better to see other than cars flying by not even noticing it. I wondered if it had a name.

'Pedro,' I shouted out. That was the first name that came to me. I stood there wondering about Pedro's life and how in fact he was probably a wolf and not a dog for the purposes of my imagination. I then turned around and started cycling off but something made me stop. I hated that Pedro was going to possibly be there forever until Spain decided to turn this road into a motorway and he'd be ground into pulp by the road diggers. That made me sad. There was only one thing for me to do, take him with me. I turned around and went back and picked up his skull. We looked at each other and I could feel his energy. I got out some cable ties and fastened him right at the front of Miss Moneypenny so that he'd get the best view. I had no idea if I'd be allowed across borders with a dead dog, I mean wolf, attached to my bike but I'd cross that bridge when I got there. For now he was coming with me until someone told us otherwise.

I pushed forward in high spirits even though my two mascots, Little Flying Cow and Pedro, weighed in total 345g which is almost the exact weight I chose to get rid of by not bringing a tent. To save 350g I opted for a bivvy instead of a tent. Mascots or tent. In the past I've always regretted not taking a tent but each and every time I still choose to leave a tent behind on fast bike rides to save weight. I promised myself to revisit that question at the end of this adventure but for now I was happy with my setup.

By 11pm I had done 182 miles and decided to get some sleep. I wasn't tired but that had been my target and I needed to play the long game. I found a woodland just off the road and tucked myself under some trees to avoid any overnight dew. Luckily the moon was bright which meant I didn't have to use my head torch which could raise suspicions from the farmhouse nearby. I presumed this was his woodland and although he probably wouldn't have minded letting a smelly cyclist sleep here, he would not know that to be the case when he saw a head torch foraging around. He'd most definitely come and investigate, probably with a shotgun. This interaction would inevitably cost me valuable sleeping time which I couldn't afford to lose.

My bivvy sadly made sleeping far too hot so I used it as a groundsheet instead. This meant that I needed to be out in the elements. Again, with my 15 minute self-imposed time limit, I wolfed down 5 small chorizo sticks, a bag of crisps and tucked in for the night. Before I put my ear plugs in and pulled a buff over my face I checked to see where Jonas was. He was about 70 miles behind me. With any luck he wouldn't be too far ahead of me when I woke up in the morning.

Pedro

Race Time: 2 Days. 11 Hours. 30 Minutes
Location: Cuellar, Spain
Miles Cycled: 412

I awoke suddenly at 4am. I had a terrible sleep, the chorizo giving me a thumping heart rate as my muscles tried to use the protein to repair themselves. It was also sweltering. I had to take all my clothes off in the night and even still I was soaking wet. Now that I was up, I checked where Jonas was. Blimey, he was literally on top of me. It's as if subconsciously he had woken me up by riding past me. I got up immediately with a new vigour as it's likely I'd catch him fairly early on and that excited me. The initial goal was to be able to get far enough ahead of him that he was unable to catch me in the night. I figured this may take a few weeks but it gave me something to chase and in turn would buy me some time.

It was at around 6am that my stomach started to rumble. I desperately needed the toilet. I had been sluggish all morning but often found that once I had rid myself of the infestation caused by copious amounts of milkshake, crisps and chorizo, I tended to fly along.

Luckily a service station not far ahead helped me with my needs and I followed it up with a huge coffee and a cake. In doing so I started what would become my morning ritual. A ritual that over the next 3 weeks became of the utmost importance - searching for the Three C's.

'I am a cycling God,' I shouted aloud. Today was the day to attack. I'd slept well, eaten and hydrated perfectly, had my Three C's, felt quite motivated and muscles didn't feel an ounce of pain. I stepped it up a gear and allowed the road to fall behind me and the Spanish countryside to whiz by in a blur. As beautiful as the medieval forts and misty vineyards were, sightseeing was for tourists and a tourist I was not, not today.

Attack, attack, attack, is all I was thinking all morning and I was doing well for the first few hours before things started to fall apart. I've mentioned the Five Pistons of Endurance to allow big miles and today I had all five ferociously firing away, never missing a beat. These are the things that I could control, for the most part anyway. But there are also a few other elements that can stop you from doing big miles and they are what I call, fairly uncreatively I'll admit, 'Show Stoppers' and are often out of your complete control.

When planning any long endurance record or adventure I always think of all the things that can happen which would make me fail at my attempt. For this Europe record these included: injury, a spoke break, tyre failure, frame break, illness, getting run over, falling asleep on the bike, road quality and lastly, bad weather. I needed to have everything in place to limit these 'Show Stoppers' from happening. To avoid injury, I needed to do more injury avoidance training and make sure my 'muscle management' was in order during the ride. I needed spare spokes and a spare tyre. I went with a steel frame. I had some vitamin tablets and would make sure I ate some healthy food. I had bright clothing, 6 rear lights, and reflective tape on my rear stays, crank arms and the back of my shoes along with a cut up hi-viz jacket at the back of my pannier. I had Pro-plus and caffeine tablets. For road conditions this involved spending hours on Google street view to see if the route I had chosen was good enough to do big miles. Lastly, when it comes to weather I know what you're thinking, you can't do anything about this, but you can. The Europe record can be done in both directions so I could have started in Russia. This way you have the option of general wind direction. For the most part Europe has westerlies so starting in Portugal made more sense. Also, there are better times of the year for better weather. The end of April seemed the best, before it became too hot in the summer.

All that said, these 'Show Stoppers' are often out of your control. A spoke can break anytime, there can be roadworks and/or a diversion, and the wind could decide that it wanted to do a 180 and blow directly from the north-east, which is exactly what happened to me at around 10am – a killer of a headwind. It wasn't just blowing, it was BLOWING! My pace went from a blistering 18mph down to around 7mph. Apart from being emotionally draining, my planned food stops that had been 2 hours apart were now 4 hours apart and with an hour and a half still to go, I completely ran out of all supplies.

To add insult to my situation the road I was on was a main truck route across Spain. The wind from trucks flying past would either push my front wheel off the road (the one downside with having aero wheels), or suck me back into the road in line with the second truck that hadn't seen me. On one occasion the gust pushed my wheel off the road and into the dirt. The gravel had been compacted enough previously for me to ride it out and then get back onto the blacktop once the trucks had passed. This time the wheel sunk into soft sand and slid off down the bank. This made my body fall directly into the road. It all happened so fast and I was fully expecting to hit my head on the road and for it to be shortly flattened by 18 wheels, but I somehow managed to unclip my shoe and skid my cleats along the ground to avoid landing in the road. I immediately pulled off the road and got off the bike.

'You're ahead Sean. Don't push it and make bad decisions. Less haste, more speed,' I said to myself. It was true. The 222 miles in the first 24 hours had allowed me some breathing space. I got back on Miss Moneypenny and continued the slog.

The wind was unrelenting all day until 6pm and I only managed a meagre 115 miles in a dismally slow 14 hours. I had reached the town of Soria and decided to treat myself to a full hour's dinner break and look at my route ahead.

As with most adventure racing, big mile cyclists will admit an unhealthy affinity to fast food that in the real world they would almost certainly turn their noses up at. The thing with fast food is that all the bits that are normally bad for you, are pretty good for cycling a long way and the food comes quickly too. Tonight was no different as I managed to find a Burger King and ordered 2 whopper meals with milkshakes. I sat stuffing my face for half an hour till I realised I still had my helmet on. I took it off slowly, even my arms ached from spending all day hunched over on the aero bars. I looked at the route ahead. I was still ahead of Jonas but he had started cycling and by the looks of things he had a tailwind on this section and was gaining fast. The headwind had pushed me beyond tired and fatigue but I needed to push on. The problem was that I was heading north up into the mountains. The climb looked like it would take 2-3 hours which meant I would need to sleep high up in the cold. I wasn't sure I had the right sleeping bag for that. It was likely to be treeless so finding shelter would be hard and finding food impossible as there wasn't anything until way down the other side, possibly 4 hours away. I had 2 options. Stay the night here, rest up but suffer a really short day which could take me up to a week to claw back, or cycle on slowly which would take me a few hours longer in my current state and then potentially have an awful night's sleep which would hinder tomorrow, but at least I'd get more miles in today. It was a tough decision as Jonas was closing in on me by the second. This route north was the one section I didn't know either. The previous year I had gone east and around these mountains but it had been a terrible choice. The road was busy with tons of trucks and constant roadworks sending me down dirt tracks. This was the only other option and seemed the slightly better one. If only I had reached here at midday instead of early evening. The headwind was having a disastrous knock-on effect on my logistics.

I really didn't know what to do, but after much thought I decided to sleep where I was and get up at 4am to tackle the hill, hopefully feeling fresh. I cycled out of town, checked into a cheap hotel and was soon fast asleep.

Finding the flatlands of Spain

Race Time: 3 Days. 10 Hours. 0 Minutes
Location: Soria, Spain
Miles Cycled: 530

4am came around as if I had been asleep for only 10 minutes. I felt completely refreshed and put my stinking clothes back on.

'Dammit, why hadn't I washed them? I always said I'd stay in a hotel once a week and wash my clothes using the free shampoo and I wish I had done that last night. It was unlikely I'd be in another hotel for some time.

I checked the tracking map and as I had guessed Jonas was miles ahead of me, maybe 80 or so. The worst part was that it looked like he had passed me before midnight which means he was around 2 hours ahead of me. Although I knew this would happen, I felt depressed. Most Tour de France leaders only win the tour by minutes. Jonas was hours ahead of me now. I had gone from being about 5 hours ahead to about 2 hours behind. It would take me a week to claw back those lost miles.

The climb began about half an hour into the morning's ride. It was dark and got surprisingly cold as I made my way up, so I decided to cycle faster which made my muscles burn but kept me warm. About an hour in, as I was nearing the summit, I came across what would have been a perfect camping spot, a fully enclosed bus shelter.

'Dammit Pedro, we should have continued yesterday,' I said. Had I continued I'd have found this and most certainly slept in it and not only would have had a good dry, wind-free night, but would have been ahead of Jonas at midnight. The guilt from a short day and early night far outweighed my rested body as I continued up and along the bare mountainside with the most important of all the 5 pistons, mind-set, not firing at all.

Things got even more depressing when I started the long downhill. It was 7am and the sun hadn't risen above the towering mountains to my right. I was so cold my shivers would make my front wheel wobble, which at 50mph is quite nerve-racking I can assure you. My shoulders started tensing up. My teeth were giving woodpeckers a run for their money, and bits of ice crystals started to form on my beard from the condensation of my breath.

Meandering through the mountains did somewhat help in lifting my mood, but more importantly I needed to warm up fast and counted every metre of the sun rising as it shone on the opposite mountain. At one point I was just about to get off the bike and run up the hill to reach the sunlight when I saw the slightest glimpse of warmth ahead of me. 100 metres away was the smallest of shafts of light across the road. It was only half a metre wide. I raced down and stopped right in the shaft. I was immediately blinded by the brightness and closed my eyes. I stayed on the bike but turned my head and body 90 degrees to face the sun. I could feel the warmth immediately, except for my arms which were outside of the shaft of light. I brought them in as if I was trying to squeeze through a small gap in a fence. I don't know how long I stood there with my eyes shut, but came to when a car hooted at me as they drove past.

'Allez, Allez!' I shouted angrily and threw my arms in the air. I was about half an hour away from Calahorra and breakfast. I pushed on.

The road followed a meandering river, occasionally climbing just enough to warm me up, before descending again. The sun rose quickly and I soon forgot all about being cold. I forgot too, at times, that I was in Spain. This area felt remarkably like Italy with quaint mountainous stone villages.

Rock falls were also quite a regular occurrence on this section and a few times I was sent down a makeshift dirt track while they repaired and removed hundreds of tonnes of rock from the road above. Although detours, they were never long enough to impact greatly on my progress. Pedro, Little Flying Cow and I thought of them as mini adventures. At least there hadn't been one overnight because the detour could be catastrophic to my daily target.

What I only later discovered was that about half an hour after I passed that section there had been another huge rock fall and had I not made it through, I would have had to climb all the way back up and down to Soria and taken a longer route around. That detour would have cost me nearly 8 hours.

Calahorra came into view at around 9am where I stocked up on food and water and continued northwards towards the ever-looming Pyrenees and the point at which I gave up last year. Today was an important day for me.

With the long downhill in the morning, a tailwind and some flat farmlands I was able to keep a good average pace and claw back some of the time I had lost to Jonas. Breakfast number 2 at around 11am consisted of a banana, chorizo and a frozen pizza which I lay in the sun for 10 minutes to defrost before eating. I nearly vomited as I tried to stuff the dry, uncooked base and still frozen bits of cheese down my throat.

It wasn't until nearly 3pm when I eventually passed Jonas, a full 2 hours later than the previous day. And to think he had been literally on top of me when I started cycling 2 days before. My lead was all but lost and the huge effort to do the 222 miles at the start appeared at this stage to have been all in vain. I should have perhaps saved the energy, but hindsight is wonderful. If I'd had a tailwind yesterday, things would be very different now. I just needed to sort my act out and keep pushing.

The Pyrenees too were encroaching, almost suffocating. Beyond those mountains lay unknown territory. Up till now I knew what the roads were like, had remembered where to get food and when big climbs were approaching. This information had been invaluable, but once in France, the next 3,200 miles would be where the real challenge started. My advantage was all but over and I had not capitalised on it at all.

My route headed about 20 miles east of Pamplona and up over the Col Ibaneta. It seemed this was one of the only passes open. The late snow in April had kept many of the smaller back road passes closed, the passes that I had planned on taking. I was now going to have to take a much bigger and busier road which wasn't really an issue going up, but bombing down alongside big trucks, which I would often go faster than, was a lot more dangerous. There was no point allocating much thought to it though, it was my only option.

I veered east and took the narrow back roads out and around towards the small village of Urroz. I couldn't help but think back to the previous attempt. It had been along these last few miles where I had battled the most. Physically my leg was in pain and I had no power but what was even more painful was the concept of quitting. This was because my injury wasn't quite bad enough to stop me altogether. It was just bad enough to reduce my mileage to 150 miles per day. With the injury not getting any better I soon fell way below the record pace. I remember reaching Urroz and settling into a cafe. I sat there for 2 hours staring into a cold cup of coffee, slowly realising that I couldn't carry on. Tears rolled down my face, the realisation of failure was unbearable. I turned away from passers-by so as not to invoke conversation. I just wanted to be alone, disappear and not have any questions. Eventually I decided I couldn't carry on and turned left at the crossroads and went into Pamplona where I slept for 2 days.

I was now back at those exact crossroads. Straight ahead was the record, the dream, the goal I had worked so hard for, and to my left was failure. I stopped briefly and looked down the road I had taken and felt sad for the old me. I felt sad, as if that Sean hadn't been me at all. Kind of like watching someone else fail at something. It was a strange feeling. I turned away and looked ahead. This was it. The long climb up and over the Pyrenees and into France. I wasn't sure if I was ahead or behind the record but didn't care to work it out. I just needed to keep cycling.

'Yeeehaaaaa!' I shouted as I remounted Miss Moneypenny, punched my arm in the air and darted over the crossroads and into unknown territory.

The climb started off very gently and I was joined by a Spanish cyclist who was doing his regular 45-mile loop from Pamplona. His English was pretty basic and my Spanish non-existent, but we managed to survive and get along nicely for over an hour. The company made the time fly by and we eventually reached the main road that would take me up and over Col Ibaneta. He turned left and went back to Pamplona. I turned right and started the real climb.

Apart from some short, sharp hills in Spain this was my first proper hill climb and my legs felt it. My quads were heavy and for the first time I considered ditching Pedro. I almost heard him snarl at me so decided to keep him. Instead I got off the bike and used a crash barrier to roll my thigh. I can't apologise enough for what it must have looked like to passing cars as I rolled the front of my quads up and down the smooth rounded bulges you get in crash barriers. But hell did it work. It's as if I had been given a shot of caffeine, Red Bull and adrenalin all at once as I floated up the hill.

'Must remember Muscle Management Sean,' I said to myself. And it was true. I hadn't been firing on all pistons since the start of the big headwind day.

I climbed and climbed, breathing deeply but in control and then climbed some . . .? What? Why was I at a crest with a brown summit sign saying Ibaneta 1057m? Was this really the top? Surely it couldn't have been? I had thought the Pyrenees would go at least to around 2,000 metres. 1,000 metres really was not high at all, I mean the hill outside my house is 800m and I don't consider Coniston Old Man to be anywhere near Pyrenean awe and grandeur.

As it turned out I had conquered the Pyrenees and was soon bombing down the other side as the sun was setting. My target for the night was the famous Saint-Jean-Pied-de-Port, the town where many intrepid wanderers start the Camino de Santiago trail. I was just nearing the bottom when I got a message on my phone. It was from my friend Tobias who I, along with the now formidable Ross Edgley, did a Tough Mudder together back in 2014 and have remained friends ever since. Tobias now lives in the Pyrenees and was on his bicycle coming to find me.

'I'm on my way to St-Jean-Pied-de-Port to meet you. Found some hostels for 15 Euro. Should arrive by 10pm.'

He followed it up later with another message that simply said, 'Wet.'

This side of the mountains, the French side, feels like a different planet. The Spanish side was dry, harsh and brown but the French side green and practically tropical in comparison. Tobias had got caught up in one of the many evening storms but was slogging on, regardless.

Being the bustling traveller town that it was, meant that every hostel was closed and the only place open was a hotel down by the river. After some food we checked in and it wasn't until we had unpacked everything that we found out our bikes were to be locked in a store room and would only be unlocked when the new manager came in at 7am! 7am! That was near on 3 hours after I normally woke up.

'Come on mate. You'll beat the record by more than 3 hours. I know you will,' Tobias said giving me some encouragement.

'And if you don't you can blame me,' he laughed. I don't think he was taking this record as seriously as I was.

'I guess so. Maybe a good sleep is what I need,' I replied but it was more to make him feel better. This would put me 5 hours behind Jonas and would result in a short day tomorrow.

At the crossroads where I gave up the previous year

Race Time: 4 Days. 12 Hours. 30 Minutes
Location: Saint-Jean-Pied-de-Port, France
Miles Cycled: 695

My alarm went off at 6.30am and I was ready within 10 minutes. Tobias faffed around a bit and all I remember thinking was he'd make a rubbish big mile cyclist. But it didn't matter because we couldn't get our bikes till 7am anyway so I let him faff away as I stared out of the window at the morning light. I hadn't woken up in daylight once during this ride and I felt extremely guilty for it.

Tobias speaks fluent French and moved from London to the Pyrenees a couple of years previously. He married a South African girl who in the strangest of coincidences, grew up on the same street as I did. I lived at number 1 and she down at number 29 or something, but we never met. It was great to catch up with Tobias and find out how to do fast miles in France, where to get food, and what to look out for.

'Boulangeries mate. They usually open early, 5am sometimes. That's what you need to look for,' he said.

'Also, remember France closes from 12 till 2pm and almost everything is closed on Saturdays, Sundays and often Mondays too,' he continued.

'What day is it today?' I asked, genuinely not knowing what it was.

'Saturday mate.'

'Ah, it's probably going to take me 3 days to get across France and you're saying everything will be closed?' I asked.

'Probably, except boulangeries.'

'Right.'

It was a beautiful morning. The temperature was perfect, the roads quiet and the low-lying mist blanketing the green pastures calmed my often agitated mood when trying to catch Jonas each morning.

We did a fast 50 miles before stopping for some food. I grabbed 4 croissants, a coffee and decided to take the opportunity to put more air in my tyres while Tobias ran off to draw some cash; he said breakfast was on him. My tyres had been a bit softer than I had wished and were therefore more likely to get a pinch flat, or 'snake bite' as they're called. It's when your wheel hits a rock and the rock pushes the inner tube against the rim which then punctures it with 2 long snake bite looking holes. They are almost impossible to patch properly. The best way to avoid them was to add more air to the tyre which would stop it compressing. I used Tobias's pump as it was a bit bigger and gave a good 50 or so pumps until my shoulder hurt. I then unscrewed the pump and as it came to the end, the entire tube deflated with a huge puff. I looked at the nozzle valve and saw that it had completely unscrewed. I couldn't understand. I didn't even know inner tube valves had an end that could be unscrewed. What happened was the tightness of the pump was tighter than the valve itself. I pulled it out and tightened it back onto the stem with my fingers and pumped it up again. This time from empty it took at least 300 goes. I had to stop several times and swap arms. It was killing me. I then unscrewed the pump but again the unscrewing of the pump unscrewed the nozzle off the stem and all the air came rushing out. This was not good. I only had one new inner left as I hadn't fixed the last one yet. I needed to find a way of screwing in the nozzle onto the stem of the inner tube tighter than I could with my fingers. I needed pliers but didn't have any. I looked up and then something caught my eye. Pedro's fangs were right at my eye level. Teeth. That's what I need to do. Not Pedro's of course, my own. Maybe I could bite the nozzle closed. I had to try. I spun the tyre until the nozzle came around to my head height and then, like a calf suckling milk from its mother, I bit onto the nozzle valve and turned my head sideways. It was turning, only slightly but that was enough. It just needed to be tighter than the pump. I was just finishing off when Tobias came back.

'What are you doing?'

'Um, nothing.'

'All you ultra-chaps are the same. No social awareness. You can't be doing that sort of thing to your bike, not in public anyway,' he joked.

'You can talk Mr MDS,' I replied, reminding Tobias that he is a serious ultra-runner himself and once was the fastest Brit in the Marathon Des Sables, a 140-mile run through the Sahara.

'Fair point,' he said and then looked at my flat tyre.

'Oh bollocks. You got a flat, when did that happen?'

'Na, just tried to put more air in and let it out instead.'

'You plonker.'

'I know.'

I then went through the whole shoulder wrenching 300 pumps again, sweating and swearing, until the tyre was rock hard. I slowly unscrewed the pump and this time it worked and we were ready to carry on.

At early lunch in Orthez it was time for Tobias to turn right and cycle back toward Pau. He showed me to a boulangerie and we ordered 2 slices of pizza each and sat on the floor of the carpark in the sun devouring them with absolute zero social awareness and it was glorious.

It had been great to cycle with Tobias and trying to keep up with his lightweight race bike helped me gain an hour on Jonas. I looked at my map and my goal for the day was hopefully going to be Bergerac. I had some logistics to consider because tomorrow was Sunday and for the most part everything would be closed. I'd also likely only reach Bergerac after everything had closed this evening too, so my best option was to sleep this side of the town and hope a boulangerie would be open first light. Google suggested there were quite a few in the town and one of them that wasn't too far off course opened at 6am. A quick scan of satellite view showed a nice little forest 5 miles out of town and that would bring my daily total to around 180 miles, which was good enough.

Even with the hour I gained it still took me till nearly 4pm before I overtook Jonas. It seemed he too had had a good day on this section.

By early evening I reached the town of Marmande and settled in for a proper sit-down meal of lasagne and decided to have a pint for no particular reason. If I'm honest I kind of ordered it by mistake but it came and I drank it as if my life depended on it. It didn't even taste good, it was a lager. Nevertheless, calories are calories, right.

To get out of town I also landed up cycling down a one-way street and had to bunny hop onto the pavement as a car hooted at me and then an uproar of lads in a bar all jeered and shouted 'Forrest Gump' at me. It was all good natured though, except the driver, he genuinely hated me. 5 seconds later I cycled right through the middle of the biggest dog turd I have ever seen and heard it flick up onto my frame and rear pannier bag. It stank and I put it down to bad karma for cycling down the one-way street.

With the wetter climate of western France came the most annoying of all creatures, the midge. There were millions everywhere. At early dusk, when it was still bright enough to wear my sunglasses it was fine but it soon became too dark, so I took them off and hoped for the best. Within 100 metres I was blinded in both eyes by at least three midges stuck on the inside of my eyelids. It felt like someone had inserted a strip of sandpaper that was now scratching my eye every time I blinked. The only respite was to close my eyes. I stopped and frantically pulled my eyelashes away from my eyeball and moved my eyes around. It didn't work. I then licked my index finger, pulled the eyelash away again and began wiping my eyeball as if my finger was a windscreen wiper. I don't know what was worse for me, having grubby fingers in my eyes, or in my mouth. Either way I kind of managed to get the midges out of my right eye but not my left. I decided to carry on cycling with one eye. I went another 100 metres and again my one open eye got filled with midges. It was impossible to carry on. I repeated my eyeball windscreen wiper technique which allowed one eye open and decided to put my sunglasses back on. Everything went dark. I could just about make out what was on the road when my bike light was on. I decided to tilt the light a bit lower to give more light in front of me. This would allow me to avoid rocks and potholes. Annoyingly the road was fairly quiet and for the first time I wished for more cars so that their headlights would help light up the road ahead.

This all lasted about an hour before it really became too dark and dangerous to cycle with my sunglasses on so I took them off and squinted for another half hour before most of the midges had gone to bed.

Because of my late start it took me till 11.30pm to reach my little woodland where I found a perfect spot on some dry leaves and was soon fast asleep.

Cycling with Tobias

Race Time: 5 Days. 11 Hours. 0 Minutes
Location: Bergerac, France
Miles Cycled: 865

It was 5am when my alarm went off and besides a mouse scuttling over me at some point in the night I had the most incredible dreamless, soundless sleep. It was so deep that I didn't even wake up when my camping mat completely deflated in the night. I seem to have picked up a small puncture somewhere. I would have fixed it there and then but I just wanted to get on the bike so I decided to fix it at a lunch stop later on in the day.

Things got even better when I found a boulangerie that opened at 6am and I bought all the pizza I could fit in my belly and stuff into the back of my jersey, some cake and a coffee.

Bergerac came and went, and apart from scrambling up a slippery bank to join a different road that I should have been on, things went smoothly. An hour later I happened upon a Sunday market and stocked up on 3 large home-made duck sausages. I presumed they were duck because when I pointed at the ones I liked the look of, the butcher man said quack-quack and waved his elbows and then laughed when I pretended to waddle on the spot.

Besides having the best sleep and a slightly more interesting than usual breakfast choice, today was a big day because I was going to reach the 1,000 mile mark. With any luck I'd reach it by midday which meant I would be a whole 9 miles per day further than Jonas. I know that doesn't sound a lot but I can assure you, at the end of a long day, 9 miles feels like 90 miles. Practically though, once you include stops, traffic lights, a few hills and buying food, 9 miles can equate to about an hour, so by the looks of things I had built up a nice 6 hour lead on Jonas.

Happy in the knowledge I had a 6 hour lead, I immediately lost an entire hour as I, all of a sudden, became the world biggest faffer. I seemed to be stopping every mile or so for various reasons. Cycle a mile. Shoelace tapping on crank causing annoying click. Stop. Re-tie lace to side of foot. Cycle 2 miles. Get too hot. Stop. Take off jersey and thermal layer. Cycle 1 mile. Get too cold. Stop. Put thermal layer back on. Cycle half a mile. Drop water bottle while trying to put it back in cage in tri-position. Stop. Turn around and pick up water bottle that's now rolled half way down a muddy bank. Cycle 50 metres. Stop. Take mud from bank scrambling out of cleat because it's not clicking into the pedal properly. Cycle 100 metres. Stop. Take a photo of some cows mating. Cycle 1 mile. Realise I haven't brushed my teeth in days which is ridiculous considering my toothbrush is velcroed to the aero bars right in front of me. Don't stop, but slow down significantly to brush my teeth. See blood in my spit. Stop. Check gums in bike mirrors. Carry on cycling hoping they do tooth replacements on the NHS . . . and so on. Limiting time off the bike is often far more effective than trying to cycle fast. Today I was doing neither.

The other thing I was trying to do was to look back at Jonas' Instagram to give me any tips about the route ahead. He sadly didn't post much but the post that I think related to today or possibly tomorrow said he only cycled 149 miles. His post read: *Greetings from France! Toughest day so far and struggled a lot in the hills this afternoon. Now feeling better and still on the bike. Will end the day at 240 km today and am almost halfway across France.*

Hills I was not expecting at all. In fact, I had presumed the exact opposite. I thought most of France, this far northwest anyway, would be as flat as a pancake, but if Jonas only did 149 miles then there must be some serious hills ahead.

Other than the annoying click from the end of my shoe laces hitting my crank on each revolution and my bleeding gums, I also had to deal with my shirt and shorts which were now completely salt sodden. They barely moved in the wind and I'm convinced if I took them off they'd be as rigid as a sheet of steel.

When salt clogs up your clothing, it A, stops them breathing so you sweat more, and B, it stays wet and never really dries out in the significantly more humid France. Spain had been much dryer so I hadn't noticed the salt situation as much. This meant I hadn't paid much attention to it and that in itself was my undoing. Not only is it uncomfortable, but the salt in my shorts creates something along the lines of very fine sandpaper and sores begin to form on the pressure points. The dirt and salt then gets into these sores and causes a cyst, or blister. Untreated they can become infected and could end the record attempt. Ocean rowers have the same problem. Usually by the time you actually realise you have these sores, it's almost too late. Prevention is far better than cure.

I immediately regretted not taking every moment to wash my kit when I could have, in rivers, fountains or in that hotel with Tobias. I knew I wasn't going to stay in a hotel again till maybe Switzerland so I really needed to make a plan, fast. In the meantime, I'd need to find some baby wipes.

The hills Jonas had complained about soon materialised and they were the worst type of all. At about 1 mile it took about 5 minutes to climb up each one, but only 1 minute to descend. 5 minutes up. 1 minute down. All morning. It basically felt like I was climbing all day and my overall average pace dropped to well below 10 miles per hour. On top of the slow progress it was also Sunday and everything in France was closed, and not just Sunday closed. Many shops looked closed for good, shutters down and not a person in sight. Maybe it was a French thing. Were they all down in St Tropez sunning themselves or on strike or something? It was eerie cycling through almost deserted villages. After the 5th closed shop my fascination turned to panic because I was running out of food. There were a few bigger towns off course but I couldn't afford to leave my planned route. Even a 5 mile diversion would cost me an hour. So I struggled on for 2 more hours, my stomach spasming with pain, my tongue so dry it started sticking to the roof of my mouth. After the 2 longest hours of my life I eventually reached both food and the 1,000 mile mark in the town of Ussel. I was emotionally and physically drained.

Not only was the 1,000 mile mark a significant milestone for being a quarter of the way, but it also allowed me to open one of my letters from Caroline. She wrote me one for each 1,000 miles cycled. I found a quiet park bench and read it to myself and immediately started crying. I had no control of the tears running down my face. We had just got engaged and were to be married a few months after I (hopefully) completed this ride. I was emotional because the letter said that I needed to stay safe on the road and come back alive. Tears clogged up my eyes as I thought the unbearable thought of Caroline getting a message that I had been knocked off the bike. I wrapped the letter back up in the plastic bag again so it wouldn't get wet and composed myself.

'I will get to the end and if I do it quicker, that's less time on the roads,' I said out loud.

It was true. If I managed to take a few days off the record, that's a few less days where I could get run over on the worsening roads in Eastern Europe that I'd heard so much about.

An hour later, tears wiped away and with a belly full of strawberry milkshake, potato wedges and chicken nuggets I continued east, checking my mirrors three times as often as I had done previously to make sure no car or truck managed to sneak up on me. I now had extra vigour to get to the end quicker.

The hills never stopped and it took till 9pm to match Jonas' 149 miles. I still had some energy in the tank so I pushed on. Eventually at around 10pm, and 161 miles for the day, I found a sheltered woodland to camp. It had been a good day but the hills played havoc with my knees. I needed to loosen my quad muscles in order to stop them tightening overnight. When your quads get cold and tight, it can pull your kneecap off centre when cycling. This is called bad 'tracking' which causes friction and can eventually lead to a serious injury that could take weeks to heal. I could not afford that. I needed to massage my thighs before bed in order for them to stay relaxed overnight.

I put Miss Moneypenny up against a tree and then used her as a clothes rack as I stripped off. In my birthday suit (except for my cycling shoes), I then wandered around the forest looking for a smooth branch, all the while wondering why I hadn't in fact done this before removing all my clothes. I eventually found a suitable piece of fallen branch that was still fresh and hadn't rotted yet. It was slightly thicker than a broom handle and about a foot in length. It was rough but I managed to peel the bark off revealing the smooth slightly moist inside, the perfect tool to roll up and down my leg like you would with a rolling pin.

I rested my bare right buttock up against a tree, put the branch just above my knee and pulled up towards my hip along my quad. The pain was unbearable as my legs went weak and I slid my bum cheek down the trunk, scratching it on the rough bark as I slid down. I found my footing and repeated the process on both legs until I felt the tightness had loosened.

Whenever I do this, I think of all the times I have been starkers in a forest and the same thought crosses my mind. My thought is that someone has installed one of those owl spotting night cameras high up in the trees. Ones that start recording when they detect movement and allows people to watch the footage live on their phones. It amuses me greatly that some old twitcher gets a notification on his phone and excitedly logs onto the camera hoping to find the rarest of night owls, only to be horrified to see a naked ginger man ferociously rubbing a stick up and down his leg. In fact I'm so convinced that this has most certainly happened that I often stop halfway through and wave up into the trees.

With my legs massaged and my mind chuckling away at the idea that my video is going to land up in a garden CCTV camera advert under the heading 'People do weird stuff in your woodland, so buy our cameras' I tucked into bed and fell asleep.

Sunrise in France

Race Time: 6 Days. 8 Hours. 55 Minutes
Location: Chavanon, France
Miles Cycled: 1026

I awoke suddenly by sprinkles of water on my face. I looked at my phone, it was 2.55am. It had started to rain but my position under the tree was keeping almost all of it off me. Still desperately tired, I decided it was not raining enough to warrant me getting up, so closed my eyes again and dozed off. 10 minutes later I awoke again with a startle when a large drop of water fell right into my nostril. I listened again to hear if it was raining properly but it was difficult to hear with my earplugs in. It didn't seem that bad but I took them out just in case. As soon as the first one was out, the forest came alive with falling rain drops. It was deafeningly loud. I was surprised my earplugs had dulled out the sound at all. But

I guess it only seemed loud because there were no other sounds around as the day was yet to start.

I looked down at the bottom of my sleeping bag which was sticking out from under the tree, it was completely wet. Thankfully only on the outside and the rain hadn't seeped into the filling just yet but that was about to happen and once wet, it'd be almost impossible to dry out, let alone carrying the extra 500g it would probably weigh, making me even more annoyed for not bringing a tent.

The rain was far too hard to continue to sleep so I slowly got up and put my now even wetter clothes back on and began to cycle. In hindsight I should have done a little naked run around the forest to warm up but I didn't and the wind-chill from the long dark downhill cut me to the core.

'Cycle faster you idiot,' is all I could hear Pedro saying and he was right. If you ever get cold the best way to get warm is to go faster. So that's exactly what I did.

As tired as I was it was nice to know I was getting a good few hours in that I ordinarily wouldn't have. Jonas was still ahead of me, but it looked like I would overtake him well before midday which would give me a much-needed morale boost. Minutes, minutes, minutes. I just needed to steal minutes whenever I could and attack when all was going well. Maybe today would be that day but until I found the Three C's, which wouldn't be for a good 4 hours or so, I'd settle with keeping a steady pace of 13mph.

At 6am I reached the town of Pontemoor. Nothing was open except for a tabac where I was able to have a coffee. I couldn't find any cake so settled for three blocks of sugar in my coffee while contemplating copying three builders who were at the bar ordering a shot of rum. I couldn't quite work out if they were at the end of their shift, or just about to start it.

It was 7.30am before I eventually came across a boulangerie that was open and I stuffed my face with 4 pain au chocolat, 1 litre of apple juice and 2 bananas. My appetite had somehow returned and made me realise just how fatigued and undernourished I had been for the first 1,000 miles. I finally felt like I was getting into the swing of things. It had taken me nearly 1,200 miles but nevertheless, it was welcomed. With this new energy and a 2-hour head start on the day it seemed silly not to attack. So that's exactly what I did.

I put my one headphone back in, (I cut the other one off to avoid tempting me to use both headphones) and started listening to Tony Hawkes Round Ireland with a Fridge.

I don't remember much from the rest of the day except the realisation that taking white goods around a country was a far easier way to spend a month of your life than this big mile cycling lark. I promised myself that once the record breaking was over, whenever that may be, I'd befriend a toaster or microwave and travel somewhere with it.

I'd done my required 170 miles by early evening, although at least 3 miles of that didn't count as I detoured in a few towns to get food. I had lived on fast food or processed food for days, completely ignoring the third and often most important corner of the nutrition pie - health. This thankfully changed when I found a Chinese buffet and nearly bankrupted them as I made full use of the eat as much as you want for 20 Euros offer. They clearly have never had to feed a trans-Europe cyclist before. Luckily the staff didn't actually give two hoots how much you ate and I was soon getting a few head nods of approval every time I went and filled up my tiny plate again. They make the plates tiny on purpose. Fresh vegetables, rice, pasta, chicken, shrimps, and many other unidentifiable Chinese 'delicacies' which were probably rat or scorpion and I ate them all. It was by far the best meal I had had since the start and made me realise how important it is to have all three nutritional elements; energy, recovery and health.

The afternoon was fast as I blasted east. I was in the best mood since the start and felt strong. I felt really positive for the first time about breaking this record. Yes, up until now I had believed it possible, because you have to believe, with every ounce of your body. If you don't believe you can open the door to failure and once that door is open, it's sometimes very difficult to close. So I had believed, but now I felt that belief turning into reality. But I most certainly must not let this be an excuse to take my foot off the gas. So onwards I pushed.

I reached a solid 195 miles by the time I found a decent place to sleep. There had been farmers' fields for the last 10 miles, nowhere to settle down, so when I came upon a woodland I knew I had to take it. I was annoyed that I hadn't reached 200 miles but there was a town 5 miles ahead of me and I really needed to be there in the morning to get breakfast. If I pushed on past the town this evening, it'd be a while before I would be able to get food. And anyway, 195 miles was way above what I needed to do and I was happy with that.

The evening was warm as I moved through the damp forest feeling my cleats clogging up with mud. It was so warm in fact that after 5 minutes in my sleeping bag I was soaking wet from sweat. The problem was that I couldn't sleep outside the bag because this part of France seemed to have the world's largest mosquitoes. I needed to be covered up. Already completely naked after a twig leg rubbing session I decided the next best thing was to sleep just in the bivvy.

To avoid putting the camping mat (which still had a hole in it), directly on the floor I decided to slip it into the bivvy and then climb in. The mat fitted perfectly and I squirrelled inside. It was only when my torso was completely in that I realised I literally couldn't move at all. The bivvy was so tight around me that I felt like Gulliver tied down to the ground in Gulliver's Travels.

I squirrelled out again and decided I'd just have to put my camping mat on the muddy forest floor and deal with it later. I moved some spikey twigs away and put it back down and then slid into the bivvy. It was perfect. Not too hot, not too cold and shielded me from the mosquitoes.

10 minutes later

It turns out that a bivvy is a terrible replacement for a sleeping bag. The side where my skin touched, namely my entire back, soon became freezing cold. Much like how window glass is cold in the winter, even when you're walking around in just a t-shirt. I started to shiver. Suddenly and uncontrollably, as if my body's internal heater had been turned from hot to cold in an instant. I needed to put my shirt back on so I unzipped the bivvy, sat up and put my thermal long sleeve back on and then squirrelled back in. It was perfect.

An hour later, after no sleep at all . . .

The night temperature must have been dropping rapidly because it was far too cold to sleep. I soon needed my sleeping bag again. I got out of the bivvy, laid it back on the floor, put my mat back on top of it and reverted back to Plan A like I had done right at the beginning. It was about 1am and I still hadn't slept which was taking its toll on my mood considering I had been up since 2.55am. I started to let negative thoughts encroach my mind. I had this sudden daunting feeling that I was not prepared for this record. I hadn't trained enough. I wasn't cycling fast enough to allow for longer recovery. I started to miss Caroline and our two dogs, Millie and Shackleton. I began to wonder what the point was of all this misery. For what? An ego boost? An overexaggerated pub story to regale later in life to strangers I didn't care about? My thoughts were just about to get darker when I stopped myself.

'Snap out of it, Sean,' I said out loud and forced myself to think about what was good about the ride. The sunrises, the sunsets, the fact I was pushing myself, testing myself. The pursuit of my third and final F. It would be worth it in the end. It would. I kept repeating. It would. For Mike and Lee.

Eating frozen pizza

Race Time: 7 Days. 11 Hours. 0 Minutes
Location: Seurre, France
Miles Cycled: 1221

I tried to get up at 5am when my camping mat had deflated but I was so tired I put more air in it and snoozed for an hour longer. This would also mean that things may be open by the time I reached Seurre, 5 miles away.

My plan worked and I eventually got up, cleaned the mud out of my cleats and arrived at a boulangerie at 7.10am. It had opened at 7am. I filled my face with warm pizza, croissants, some coffee and carried on.

It was an eerie morning, the low-lying mist completely drenching me as if I had cycled through a rain storm. The droplets of water falling off my beard and onto my phone thus disabling the touch-screen, making it impossible to use my finger to navigate. Luckily the route was fairly easy and a lot flatter than it had been. It was a welcome rest for my fragile knees. With yesterday's big day I hoped to have a bit of an MOT day as I liked to call them. Not a short day but a day where I keep a steady pace, don't push too hard but just match Jonas' mileage. It's quite easy to do a shorter day after a big day, but this is a dangerous strategy. Short days take potentially weeks to claw back. I am still clawing back the miles I lost in Spain on the big headwind day where I only did 115 miles. The big days are there to help with potential bad days further on. With the impending MOT day, I desperately needed to wash my clothes as the salt build-up was now so bad my shorts were sticking to my undercarriage, as if someone had poured some honey down there. When I dared to take a peek I saw that bits of skin from my blisters and rashes were embedded into the fabric of my shorts. It really was disgusting.

I was also likely to reach Germany or Switzerland today. I wasn't sure which one I'd land up in. I might in fact not go through Switzerland at all as I hadn't quite looked at this section of route beforehand. Most of my energy and frustration went on planning routes across Eastern Europe. Germany and Switzerland, I just presumed, would be easy to blast through, especially with their multitude of bike paths and therefore needed not much attention.

At 8am I got my first nose bleed. I was surprised it took this long as I'm always prone to bleeding from my right nostril. For some reason it's a lot smaller than the left, about half the size, which means the air that rushes out of it gets funnelled and gathers speed which eventually causes the nose to bleed. This is especially prevalent when I've had a lot of milk to drink which makes my nose runny and I do the old 'snot-rocket' as many cyclists will know all about. This also adds pressure to the nostril lining which causes it to rupture.

Being so misty and wet, the bleeding just wouldn't dry out either and it took nearly an hour of me cycling firstly with my head all the way back, which made me nearly vomit as blood ran down the back of my throat. Then all the way forwards but blood ran out and dripped all over my phone. I've never known what to do with nose bleeds, back or forward? Eventually I decided blood running down my throat was better than all over my phone so cycled for half an hour more with it tilted back until it kind of dried up which also blocked my entire nasal passage.

Other than the potential of cycling through three countries today, my real goal was to try and get beyond where I thought Jonas might sleep. That would mean when I awoke tomorrow I would be ahead of him. Until now he was always ahead of me in the mornings. Today he was 20 miles ahead of me which had come down significantly in the last few days from when he had been about 80 miles ahead. The one thing I was struggling to work out was how he had reached Munich by tomorrow evening. His Facebook post said he cycled to an office to give a talk the following morning. Munich was nearly 400 miles from here so he must have done 2 monster days to get there. I can only hope that, because of the talk, he then did a short day immediately after.

At mile 60 I passed Besancon and had to divert into the town to get food, and more importantly get off the hugely busy D673 dual carriageway which I had been on

144

for over an hour. It was a big fast dual carriageway where the hard shoulder was littered with glass, exploded truck tyres, sharp metal stakes, half a sofa, and all manner of other things that I could crash into or give me a puncture. I hated it but it was still the quickest option. Diverting into the town was tediously slow with traffic lights, and trying to navigate all the small alleys was painful. But I just had to do it as I hadn't eaten for 3 hours. Since the success of the Chinese buffet, I searched and found a WOK shop and I headed straight there. The food was exactly what I needed, a huge bowl of pasta with vegetables and chicken. Whilst devouring it, I noticed a message come up on Facebook from a chap who was on his bike and trying to find me. I felt bad that he was probably missing me because I was hiding in a Chinese restaurant so I let him know where I was. Less than 5 minutes later he joined me.

'Bonjour Sean. My name is Romain,' said the young skinny legged chap in a French accent. He looked to still be in his teens.

'Bonjour. Thanks for coming to find me,' I said genuinely. It was nice to have someone to speak English to.

'Is no problem. I try to find you earlier but I see you on the main road.'

'Yes, it was faster that way.'

'I see, but it is terrible that road. When I see you on it I decide not to come find you. I don't like that road. It is dangerous.'

You know a road is bad when locals won't go near it on their bikes. I suddenly thought about the road that I got run over on in America. People said the same thing about that one. I really didn't fancy getting back on it.

'Do I need to go on it again to carry on heading east?' I asked fearing the worst, hoping for local knowledge.

'No, no. The canal is just here and goes for maybe 20km with a cycle track. You will miss the main road. It's maybe 1 or 2 kilometres longer but is better for sure,' he said smiling, happy that he had imparted some useful advice.

'Ah. Thank you. Can you show me on the map how to get there?'

'No, I can cycle with you to show you. I know a fast route.'

'Wow. Thank you,' I said again.

Even if it was 1 or 2 miles longer it would be worth it. I was sure I'd get a puncture on that main road and that would cost me more time than the extra few miles, and not to mention the constant worry about getting run over again.

We cycled out of town and it was hard to keep up with Romain in 'commuter cyclist' mode. Sprint to each traffic light. Wait 20 seconds for it to go green. Sprint to the next one. It felt like I was having a high intensity interval training session but maybe this is what I needed. I've never trained with anyone and the downfall is that my pace is often slower than maybe it could be. Your legs get into muscle memory mode where they settle into a set pace. I've always wondered if my pace could have been faster had I trained with other people in the early days. Do faster days, but then have longer recovery time. I don't know. What I do know is that the past 60,000 odd miles has me set in my ways now. I'd say 'if it aint broke, don't fix it' but maybe it is broke. I was yet to become a proper big mile cyclist, even though I was ahead of Jonas at this moment. But Russia was still looming and it could still so easily be taken away from me. Having Romain blast from traffic light to traffic light as I fell way behind certainly made me feel that my slow and steady pace with less sleep was maybe the wrong approach. As tiny as his toothpick legs were, he was fast on the bike.

We eventually crossed the bridge over the river Le Doubs and arrived at the best cycle path I think I've ever seen. Roads in the Lake District are smaller. 100 metres later there was a small gangway down to a floating pontoon on the water.

'Ah. Sorry. I need to stop,' I said over-excitedly. Romain looked at me strangely.

'I really need to wash my shirt. I have been looking for a river to walk down to for days but most have reeds or muddy banks,' I continued to the befuddled look on Romain's face.

I then took off my shirt and thermal and stood there half naked. It suddenly dawned on me that Romain might possibly be far too young to have a middle-aged hairy man strip off in front of him down a deserted canal path. I quickly turned my back and walked away down the gangway and lay on the cold pontoon and thrust my clothes into the river. I'm not sure if there is a preferred technique to getting salt out one's clothing but the 'thrash it around like a shark attack' seemed to be what I figured would be the best. I did this for a solid 3 minutes, occasionally squeezing the excess water out while giving undignified groans and grunts as I felt the salt washing away. It was strangely cleansing. I felt lighter. Romain stood there with an odd expression on his face.

After getting as much of the salt out as possible, I put the wet thermal and shirt on and wandered back to the confused Frenchman who clearly had the expression of,

'Oh dear. This Sean chap is a bit odd. I think I need to leave.'

'So this is the canal you can follow for 20km. I must go home now,' he said and we shook hands and he departed hastily and never looked back.

The cycle path was a much welcomed break from the marauding traffic on the busy main road. I could comfortably go into tri position and let my thoughts wander.

My few hours on the path did wonders for my morale especially once my shirt had dried out and I could feel it flapping in the wind again. For the past week it had been so rigid even the strongest of headwinds didn't move it an inch. The sun was out and the path wasn't overrun with mums with pushchairs like they can be back home.

The only thing that really started to annoy me were the odd occasions when roots from big trees on the edge of the path had started to rise forming annoying bumps, almost rumble-strip like. Trees, having many roots meant there was often a succession of these all in a row. I could usually see them in time to get my elbows off the aero bars and hold onto the drops to keep balance, but on 1 or 2 occasions I would get caught off guard. This usually happened when I was fighting Tutankhamen on the top of a giant inflatable marshmallow, or swimming with gorilla-like fish at the bottom of the ocean because I had somehow managed to learn to breath underwater, or any of the other weird and fantastical places my mind goes to when deep in thought. One of these root bumps happened to be in the shadow of a tree, I hit it at around 18mph and my front wheel lifted clear off the ground, projecting my elbows into the air. When they came back down, more often than not they would miss the elbow pads entirely and crash down on the hard handlebars. Not only would this make me swerve uncontrollably, often towards the river, but it also hurt like hell.

The canal ended and with bruised elbows I returned to the busy main road in search of food again. I also needed my water bottles filled up so found a bakery. A lovely old lady inside didn't speak a word of English so I just pointed at the sink I could see out back and did the 'turn on a tap' gesture to get my point across. She smiled, nodded, took my bottles and disappeared around the corner. I felt in my pocket for my wallet to buy some cake but realised I had left it on Miss Moneypenny so went back outside.

When I returned, both my bottles were full. I went to pick one up and put it back down immediately. It was boiling hot. The old lady laughed and handed over a napkin. Why had she put hot water in my bottles? That was no good to me at all. I looked inside and then realised it wasn't hot water at all. It was in fact 2 litres of filter coffee. How on earth had that communication gone so wrong I thought? She then typed 6 onto her calculator and showed me. I just kind of laughed and pointed at some cake for 2 Euros and handed her a tenner and then juggled the boiling hot bottles from hand to elbow to armpit as I went back outside to Miss Moneypenny.

Cycling back up the road I found myself chuckling away at the idea that the little old lady is going to go home to her husband and say she had the strangest chap come in, all dirty and smelly, asking for 2 litres of hot coffee for his cycle bottles. I bet she ends her story with, 'Silly British people'. I hope she does.

As much as I liked the idea of drinking 2 litres of coffee and seeing what happened I decided against it and found another café to replace the coffee with water. To this day

I still think I should have tried it. I bet I would have cycled 40 hours straight and in doing so probably gained 200 miles on Jonas. One day I shall do that experiment and let you know what happens.

As with every other day on the ride so far, my body ailed me in some shape or form. I haven't written about much of it yet because I didn't want this book to be all about me whingeing the whole time. Pain is very much just a part of everyday life in endurance sport and in itself, pain is not a bad thing. Pain is, in fact, very good for you and I think society cotton-balls us so much nowadays it makes us incapable of handling it when it does come around. Pain makes you learn your limits, makes you feel alive, makes you know you're pushing yourself. Pain makes you stronger. It's not just me who thinks so. If you search the internet there are loads of influential people who've said similar. Benjamin Franklin said; 'There are no gains without pains.' Or Mary Tyler Moor who said; 'Pain nourishes courage. You can't be brave if you've only had wonderful things happen to you.' Or my personal favourite which is; 'Being a wimp is more painful than pain itself.' Anonymous.

Today's pain that was 'toughening me up', was severe cramp in my right calf. I normally don't suffer from cramp but when it arrives unannounced, it causes havoc. Every 10 minutes or so my right calf would seize up completely. Imagine a sock 10 times too small for you getting pulled over your calf and then one large needle piercing your muscle right down to the bone. That's what it felt like. No matter what stretching I did, it kept coming back. What I really needed to do is eat more salt. I had long run out of my chia salt rocket fuel and needed to make more of an effort to add salt to everything. In the past I have done various things to get more salt in me. I have licked my sweaty forearms, often after I'd forgotten I'd put sun cream on, which nearly made me vomit. I've added salt to my water bottles and even once topped up my bottle with a bit of sea water when cycling along the coast in Croatia. Chugging salt from a shaker as if it were a shot of tequila also works wonders, anything to keep on top of my daily salt needs.

By early evening I knew I was approaching Germany, mainly because when I went through one small village there was a man playing the accordion in his second floor bedroom overlooking a roundabout, with the windows wide open. This would have been a wonderfully romantic scene as he serenaded passers-by but it was somewhat ruined by him being, from the looks of things, completely naked. I can only assume he had pants on but I cannot be sure.

My suspicions were correct (about my whereabouts, not the naked guy) when I zoomed out on the map. Germany was fast approaching, but before that I was in fact going to land up in Switzerland. My route was heading right through Basel and then along the River Rhine. I had the option of either doing the north side in Germany or the south side in Switzerland. After a quick scan of the two options the south side seemed marginally quicker. Basel was also likely to be where I was going to end up this evening. I needed to do at least 170 miles, so worked out that I'd need to get 10 miles out the other side of the city and then stay in a hotel and wash my clothes. I found one online, called them and booked the room. I now had something to look forward to.

I must have done something wrong in a previous life because it seemed the karma gods didn't want me to get to my hotel. Firstly I got a puncture and for some reason couldn't get the bloody tyre back on the rim. In 2010 I broke both my thumbs in a skiing accident and since then they are often too weak to push the tyre back onto the rim. I then have to flip the tyre around and kind of roll/pull it over the lip of the rim. This often then causes my outer layer of skin, which is usually hard from being exposed to the elements and holding the bars, to detach from the inner layer causing a blister.

Eventually, and after much swearing and heated discussion with Pedro about a tool that may do this job for me, I got the tyre on and then spent an age doing the 300 pumps needed to get enough air in it. Then I was good to go.

Half an hour later, however, I started to notice my right ankle squirrelling out of the cleat. I had the cleats that allowed for 9-degree rotation. This can help avoid knee issues. My riding style seemed to have changed because of the cramp, and now whenever I pushed down on the pedal my ankle was turning outwards, pivoting on the pedal, rather than keeping straight. This in turn was causing my knee to bend in and my hip to drop slightly. It got so bad that after an hour I joined two cable ties and tied my foot to the pedal. I'd love to say this worked but it did not. The only thing it did was to stop blood flowing to my toes, so I removed it. My only solution was to really concentrate on keeping my foot straight. If it persisted I'd need to find a bike shop and buy cleats with no rotation in them.

Then on one occasion when I was looking over my shoulder to swerve into the road to avoid an illegally parked car, my headphone cable got caught under one of the elbow pads, pulled out of my ear, and fell right into my spokes and ripped the earpiece right off. I wasted an hour faffing around while I stopped in various shops and service stations to find a new pair. Eventually I found a set at the ridiculous cost of 25 Euros, almost as much as my hotel that evening. I should have just pushed on without music but I seemed to cycle quicker when my mind was otherwise entertained. Even though my battle with Tutankhamun on the marshmallow was still raging strong, I still needed further distractions to force any negative thoughts out of my mind.

Once the sun had set, twilight brought with it the picture postcard landscapes of rapeseed fields and tractors kicking up red dust. I, however, wasn't seeing any of it because I had my eyes closed mostly due to my meeting what I can only describe as a plague of King Kong midges. They were so big that it sounded like rain hitting my helmet when I cycled through a bite of them – yes that is the official collective noun for the little bastards, a bite. Remembering what happened last time, I kept my sunglasses on and powered through, often swallowing them, because my nose was still somewhat clogged up with dried blood. Extra protein I guess.

So everything was slowing me down but I eventually made it into Basel, stopped at the best stocked service station I'd seen all trip, bought some cake and a 50g protein shake, downed it pretending it was a magic potion and then carried on. It took yet a further hour to get through the city and to my hotel where I checked in, went straight upstairs and jumped into the shower, fully clothed.

Operation laundromat was in full swing. It's amazing what a week's worth of road grit, dead badger, salt and snot rockets look like in the bottom of the shower pan. Once all my clothes were off I put them in a pile on the floor of the shower, emptied one of the two free shampoos all over them, then emptied the second one on my head and pretended I was squashing grapes while I trampled all over the clothes, occasionally flipping them over with my feet to allow more water and shampoo to sink in. Once I felt everything was as clean as it was ever going to be, I wrung them out and laid them out on a towel. I then rolled the towel up with the clothes inside as tight as possible and then stood on the towel to squeeze as much water out as I could. I needed to get them as dry as possible because I needed to sleep in them. That was the only way it could get them completely dry by the morning and avoid freezing to death.

By 11.30pm I was all tucked up in bed with my wet clothes back on and soon fast asleep.

Head down in aero position

Race Time: 8 Days. 11 Hours. 31 Minutes
Location: Basel, Switzerland
Miles Cycled: 1381

I woke up suddenly at 5.31am. Somehow, I had missed my 4am alarm. Annoyed at myself, I slowly staggered over and started packing my kit which had somehow landed up in every corner of the hotel room. My head was pounding and my heart racing faster than if I had been cycling up a steep hill. I felt like I had been hit by a bull. I was already dressed of course and, as planned, my clothes were dry and smelled heavenly.

Jonas was, as expected with my unplanned lie in, quite far ahead of me now. 30 miles or so. I knew he reached Munich today which was a 200-mile day for him and considering that he's 30 miles ahead of me, if I had any chance of getting anywhere near his camp spot I'd have to do a monster day.

Within minutes I was already downstairs making the most of the free breakfast, my headache seemingly getting worse. I suddenly realised why. It's because of the 50g of protein I had just before bed. I had what's called a protein hangover. The only way you can get rid of it is to drink a lot of water, usually the night before. This morning however I needed to fill my stomach with food and not water so the headache would just have to stay for a while.

The morning was cold and as uncomfortable as the first half an hour's sleep in wet clothes was. It was still a better choice than saving the wet kit for this morning's ride. I had all my clothes on and was still freezing to death.

My journey continued along the Rhine as the sun rose ahead of me. I had started out that morning cycling along the road, but after the 1,000th person hooted at me I suddenly realised there was a perfect bike path down the bank so did some cyclo-cross to reach it. And it was a good thing I did because I was beyond tired. The adrenalin from being on the main road had kept me awake but now on the safety of the bike path I felt my entire body fading and my eyes closing. I needed to stay awake so I put my headphone in and pressed play on my next audio book, Roald Dahl's – Going Solo. That should do the trick.

Just then I saw a cyclist ahead of me and, as every cyclist will admit, I decided to have a race with him, even though he had no idea it was a race of course. Judging by his posture he looked to be an elderly gentleman on somewhat of a town commuter bike. A part of me felt guilty that in no time at all I was going to drop him like I dropped Jason on Route 66. Even if he was a pensioner the competitive side of me wanted to 'av im'.

I went down into tri position and then moved into big ring. The race was on. There was nothing between me and him, like sticks across the path, rouge ducks or root humps so I put my head down, focussed on nothing but my feet and knees moving up and down with utmost precision and put down some heavy turns on the cranks for about 30 seconds. My speedo read 33mph. I was flying. I looked up to see how close I was to catching the old man, I was sure to be almost on top of him. I paused suddenly and stopped pedalling. I wasn't on top of him. In fact, he had gained on me.

'What's going on here Pedro?' I asked out loud. And then at that exact moment my brain, in its fatigued, protein hungover state, truly believed I had somehow stumbled upon an ex-Tour de France cyclist who was still hard as nails and fast on the bike. Who could it be? I think it could be Eddy Merckx. From afar it really could. His rounded head with greying short hair. He wasn't wearing a helmet. Eddy Merckx never wore a helmet. It was definitely him alright. As I write this, it seems ridiculous but at the time I really believed I had randomly found Eddy Merckx cycling along the Rhine. And now I wanted to catch him.

I went back down into tri position and pushed hard on the pedals, this time not looking down, but looking ahead. Eddy was obviously still a strong cyclist and I'd need to pull everything out the bag to catch him. On and on I pushed, but Eddy kept ahead of me. Damn he was strong, and on a commuter bike too. What a hero. About

100 metres ahead I saw a set of traffic lights and Eddy slowed down as he was approaching. This was my time. I'd get him at the lights and with any luck there'd be enough time for a selfie with the great man. Luckily the lights were looking after me and Eddy soon stopped. I screamed along and eventually pulled up just behind him and shouted 'Eddy?' with a somewhat questioning tone because for the first time, on closer inspection, I thought that it may not be him. I rolled up till we were side by side and my heart sank. It wasn't Eddy Merckx. Of course it bloody wasn't. It was just some old grey-haired chap doing his morning cheese and chocolate run which is what I imagine every Swiss person does. He had headphones in so hadn't heard me shout at him thankfully. It also became glaringly obvious why he was so fast and I couldn't believe I hadn't worked it out immediately. He was on an e-bike. Feeling a mixture of disappointment and stupidity, I settled back into touring mode and let fake Eddy disappear off into the distance.

I saw hundreds of 'Fake Eddy's' as I now called them throughout the commute out of Basel. Old pensioners bombing along at 30 miles per hour on motorised bicycles, half of them not wearing helmets. In fact, at a pretty conservative guess, I would put e-bikes to normal bikes at about 10 to 1. Seeing someone not on an e-bike was practically grounds for conversation, like you would when you see someone with the same dog as you. At one time there were about seven of us all waiting at a set of traffic lights and there were only 2 normal bikes, myself being one of them. I know this didn't happen but we practically gave each other a nod of recognition. A nod to say, 'well done mate, you and I are doing it the hard way. Yes we will land up at our destination a lot sweatier, and take twice as long but we will become stronger for it.' The light then turned green and we were both left in a cloud of Old Spice cologne as the pensioners raced ahead.

By mid-morning I had left Switzerland and was into Germany which had just as many e-bikes. The cycle paths for the most part were fast but the downside was they often diverted into towns instead of staying along the main, more direct roads. This was starting to annoy me because all the effort to gain 10 minutes, all but disappeared in every town as the cycle path came and went, resulting in me having to stop and look at my maps more often. Once or twice I dared cycle on the main road and not on the bike path but I have to say I've never experienced such road rage in my life. It seemed drivers, almost always in fast German cars, you know the ones, would speed up and pass even closer to the edge of the road than they would have if I wasn't there. I can only think it was to 'teach me a lesson' or to make my life as difficult as possible so that I wouldn't cycle on the road again. One or two even wound down their windows and shouted something in German to me while giving me the two fingers. As much as I hoped that giving someone the finger in Germany actually meant something like 'Have a wonderful day kind sir and thank you for reducing car traffic on the roads so that I can get to work quicker,' but I feared it did not mean this at all. Not cycling on bike paths in Germany was, all in all, a terrible experience. To be fair you can't blame them. Germany has 45,000 miles of bike paths and spends 80 million Euros a year maintaining them. With this infrastructure you can see why drivers get annoyed when you don't use the paths that they've especially built for you. From then on I decided to move back onto the paths and take a hit on my daily mileage which was annoying because Jonas had done such a big day. Jonas was of course German, and obviously knew how to better deal with the rules of the roads in Germany. He too was on home soil and would know where and what to buy at each feed stop, which he could do a lot quicker in his mother tongue and not like my way which was to point at things and type stuff into Google Translate. I would hazard a guess that his home turf advantage would see him gain about 2 hours on me over the course of my German leg. 2 hours I really couldn't afford to give away.

The one plus side of the day was I had a stonking tailwind and was able to push it hard between towns. To increase my salt intake, I also decided to eat more salty nuts. I felt the effects almost immediately, my body shouting for joy at the extra much needed sodium. I also wasn't going to the loo as much because the salt allowed the water to absorb into my muscle instead of pass right on through to my bladder. The downside, and there is always one, was that whenever I dipped my hand into the salty nuts, the end of my gloves (I had full fingers gloves to avoid sunburn) would get covered in salt. My salty fingertips would then move to my mouth and touch my lips. Repeat this all day and eventually the salt build up on my lips caused them to start to crack and blister. By early afternoon I had a crack that was bleeding right down the middle of my bottom lip. Along with my still bleeding gums, my mouth was not in a happy place. But I had a tailwind so nothing else mattered.

Germany rolled on by, mostly in a blur as I meandered past rapeseed fields, small towns and the increasingly irritating maze of bike paths. By midnight it started to rain again and after trying, and failing, to find a suitable place to camp up for the night I booked into another hotel. I had lost at least an hour in the day and now a further half an hour checking into the hotel as the night porter, an 80 year old lady in her night gown, struggled to unlock the bike shed. At times I thought she may be in fact sleep-walking.

Typical camp spot in woodlands

Race Time: 9 Days. 13 Hours. 0 Minutes
Location: Mindelheim, Germany
Miles Cycled: 1561

I overslept again. It was 7am when I woke up in a panic. Momentarily I thought I was back home and this had all been a dream. Weirdly, that dream of being back home had in fact made me feel quite sad. As much as this bike ride was hurting me physically, I still wouldn't have wanted to be anywhere else in the world.

I had a quick breakfast and hit the road. Judging by the amount of water around, it had rained heavily overnight which made me feel slightly less guilty for wasting time staying in the hotel.

My tiredness from the first week had now become fatigue. I knew this would happen but hoped it may happen nearer the end. The second half of this ride was going to push me to the limits. I knew that now. On top of the fatigue, my saddle sores were getting a lot worse. It seemed I made the rookie mistake of swapping out my wide Brooks saddle, the Cambium C17, for the much lighter race version, the Cambium C13. They're essentially the same saddle but the C17 is 17cm wide and the C13 is 13cm wide with the added bonus that the rails are carbon and not steel. The C13 is therefore 214g lighter than its C17 counterpart, a huge amount in the world of self-supported bike racing. I was now however paying for those 200 odd grams saved. The 13cm wide saddle seemed to be just that little bit thin for my backside. This meant that every mile or so I'd have to stop pedalling and get off the saddle, shake my ass in the air a lot, before sitting back down at the exact spot where it didn't hurt as much. Seeing a middle age hairy chap doing some casual twerking on a touring bike must have been quite the sight for many a passing motorist. They must have thought I was listening to some heavy dance anthems when in fact I was listening all about how Roald Dahl nearly went blind from crashing his aeroplane into the desert during WW2. Very serious stuff.

Up till now I had avoided any painkillers as they often do more harm than good but the sores became so unbearable I eventually resorted to taking some paracetamol.

At midday, Jonas still hadn't moved position from Munich and I rounded the northern suburbs and overtook him. This was a much-needed boost. I checked my tracking map every 5 minutes and each time I saw that he hadn't moved it gave me that little extra lift. His strategy was becoming clearer and clearer. He was

165

probably going to do a short day. What he probably did, and it's not a good strategy at all, as I've fallen foul to it, was to work out how far he would get in 2 days at his current average which was 160 miles per day. What he then did was tell himself he can do 200 miles to get to Munich, a big day. He will then allow himself a lie in, do the talk and then he'd only have to do 120 miles the following day to be back on track. The problem is that in order to do the big day you often overcook yourself and don't manage the 120 miles, or do them 4 hours slower than usual which has a detrimental impact on the next few days. It now looked like Jonas was only going to do a short day and that was good news. If I attacked then I'd surely gain all the valuable time I'd lost on the bike paths.

I looked back at my maps to see if there was any way of finding a shorter route. After close inspection I saw a series of back roads that cut off a huge corner. The problem was that the last 3 miles or so of this potential shortcut was a dotted white line on the map. These dotted lines are like a lottery. Sometimes they are perfect black-top and other times they aren't actually roads at all. Once when cycling around Ireland I had to carry my bike through 2 miles of swampland where, I'm guessing 1,000 years ago, there may have been an old sheep track which was still a white dotted line on the map.

I needed to decide quickly. Often the act of stopping and faffing around deciding on which route to take, takes up more time than you would have gained. Minutes, minutes, minutes remember! I decided to go for it. If this dotted line was good road quality then I'd gain about 15 minutes.

The backroads were pleasant and small enough to not have any bike paths along them so in turn, no road rage from passing drivers, who were all of a sudden very accommodating. It was still flat and I still had a tailwind. As the dotted line approached I saw that it turned from tar to gravel and my heart sank. I slowed to avoid hitting it at speed only to find it was really well compacted. I sped up a bit and seemed to be in control. I sped up even more. It may not have been black-top but I was still able to push a good average. The shortcut had worked and, in the end, bought me about 10 minutes.

Nothing much else happened for the rest of the early afternoon other than the funniest sign in the middle of someone's front lawn. It was a hand-painted totem pole type sign cut out of thick plywood with 4 characters on it. The top one was a tractor. The one below it was a full litre glass of beer, the German type with a handle on the side. Below that was a vintage Vespa scooter and then lastly at the bottom was a Bavarian beer maids' outfit. Not the maid herself. Just a cut-out painted version of the typical outfit you can imagine Bavarian maids wear. Those are the four things I guess the man enjoys in life. I also guess he is probably single.

My attack day then came to an abrupt end. I was fast approaching the end of Germany and was about to begin the long climb up to the Czech border, when I noticed my phone wasn't taking charge anymore. This was by far the more serious issue, because without a phone I'd have no way of navigating or taking the relevant photos of significant landmarks that I'd need to submit to Guinness to prove my whereabouts. Fixing an electrical issue was going to be hard to pinpoint and could take me hours just to diagnose, let alone fix. It could be a problem with any one or more of any of the following:

The dynamo itself.

The connectors that attach to the dynamo which often rust and break from taking them on and off every time you get a puncture and have to remove the front wheel.

The cable from the dynamo to the voltage regulator.

The voltage regulator itself.

The cable from the voltage regulator to the battery bank.

The connection where the cable enters the battery bank which can get clogged with dust and water.

The battery pack itself.

The charging cable from the battery bank to my phone.

The place where the charging cable goes into the phone which can also get clogged with dust and water.

My phone itself could have a fault.

The first and easiest to check were the cables themselves. I had backups of all of them. I had in fact brought 5 iPhone charging cables and 3 micro-USB cables too. I decided to change these on the move so for the next half an hour I cycled a bit, swapped out various cables, cycled a bit more, realised nothing changed, swapped another cable, and carried on, eventually to no avail. Meanwhile I had to put Roald Dahl on pause and switch my phone to flight mode to save power.

At my next food stop I managed to work out that my battery bank was sending charge to my phone but it wasn't receiving it. This was bad news. A battery bank I could replace, the dynamo or voltage regulator I couldn't.

By 8pm I was nearly 160 miles in and just about to start the long climb toward the Czech Republic. For my own sanity I decided to forget about my charging issues and deal with it tomorrow. I had just about enough power to last me another 12 hours without Roald Dahl. By then I'd hopefully be able to buy a USB wall plug which in my haste I had forgotten to bring with me. It was going to be a long slog this evening having to deal with my own thoughts again, but on the plus side, I still hadn't beaten Tutankhamun on the giant marshmallow yet and was going to enjoy revisiting that feud.

The climb started annoyingly quickly straight out of Deggendorf. I pushed hard in my easiest gear, my cadence down at around 30. I could see the top ahead and didn't stop till I eventually reached it. I stopped for a breather to see my progress.

'Noooooooo!' I shouted immediately. I had somehow taken the wrong road out of town and had climbed this huge climb for nothing. I thought is seemed quieter than I had imagined the main road to the Czech Republic would have been. What's even worse is I had to go back down it to join the road I should have been on. This little mess-up not only cost me about half an hour but it also completely knackered my legs.

Back down I went, swearing all the way, and re-joined the correct road and started the climb all over again. The hill was long, hours long in fact. My legs were knackered and weak. Miss Moneypenny somehow felt 100 times heavier than she had done before the start. I was struggling to do much more than 5mph.

This climb which I hadn't actually paid much attention to in the lead up, turned out to be the hardest climb of the ride so far, putting even my Pyrenees section to shame. It may have been partly due to my fatigue but nevertheless it nearly ruined me. By 10pm I decided to stop for the night. It was an earlier than normal stop because I wanted to switch my night-time hours to starting before sunrise when the roads were quieter as opposed to after sunset when statistically more drivers may be under the influence. I guessed being on the road from 10pm onwards was looking for trouble. This was going to be at its worst when I reached Russia. About 30,000 people a year die on Russian roads, and I wanted to make sure I would be cycling when there were the least number of cars around. So, as of tomorrow, I would set my alarm for 3.58am. Having it 2 minutes before 4am made it sound like I was getting up far earlier, which was good for my mind-set.

Luckily it was forested at the top of the mountain, which it often isn't, and I was able to sneak off the road when I saw a gap in the traffic. I had to plan this incognito exit from the road in advance because I needed to turn off all my bike lights so that I wouldn't be seen. The problem was that my dynamo lights had some sort of small internal battery which kept the lights on for about 2 minutes. Not at full brightness of course, but bright enough to be seen wandering a forest. So I'd stop on the side of the road, pretend I was reading my maps or drinking and turn off my lights. I'd then wait a minute before heading into the trees, often covering up my light with my gloves which I had taken off already, in preparation for bed.

This usually happened smoothly and tonight's camp spot I have to say was one of the best. Dense pine forest with soft dry ground meant I only needed to go 20 metres off the road and I'd be out of sight. Although the ground was good I still picked Miss Moneypenny up just in case I rolled her over a thorn or such, which I have done in the past. There is nothing more annoying than waking up raring to go only to find you have a flat tyre.

I walked through the forest slowly, taking care not to stand on any sticks which might snap and give away my position. In my mind this was important and I was doing it out of habit, because in reality no car would ever hear a twig snap this far in. Suddenly my left leg disappeared and I fell to the ground. My immediate thoughts were bear trap and I was about to be impaled and come to a splintery end. Luckily the hollow wasn't that deep, thigh high perhaps, and my fall came to an abrupt and thankfully undramatic end. Out of the bear trap I scrambled and found a suitable tree to lean Miss Moneypenny against and set up camp. My mat still had a hole in it but I was finding it actually quite useful. It seemed its deflation time was around 4-6 hours which was around the time I needed to sleep. So it was in fact my backup alarm clock. If I somehow didn't wake with my alarm after 5 hours, which had been my average sleep time, then I'd awake an hour later with my butt hitting the ground. It was genius and the concept alone was enough for me not to get annoyed with it anymore.

Feeling good heading for the Czech Republic

Race Time: 10 Days. 9 Hours. 58 Minutes
Location: Zwiesel, Germany
Miles Cycled: 1730

I initially woke up at 3am but decided to stick to my 3.58am strategy so dozed until my alarm sounded. It had been a cold night. Earlier my toes had been so cold I decided to put my gloves on the ends of them which I hadn't expected to work at all, but it did. Toes a lot warmer, I was able to get a good night's sleep.

I first looked to see where Jonas was and amazingly I was ahead of him.

'We're ahead Pedro. We're ahead,' I shouted. This was it. I had woken up ahead of Jonas for the first time and it had only taken me 1,700 odd miles to do so. It also looked like he was going to stop for the day at the Czech border. I was likely to pass the border at 5am. It seemed he was going to reach there at around 9am and then sleep till about 4pm. So his big push to Munich had worked in my favour. By 4pm when he would be due to leave the border I would be about 120 miles ahead of him. This was the best news and I proceeded to do a little naked dance around the forest for the CCTV cameras.

With my mood high, I very nearly forgot all about my phone charging issues. I needed to get a wall plug by midday when I was likely to run out of power. I would then lose another hour charging my phone. Luckily my 120 mile lead gave me some much needed breathing space.

Things were looking up when I found a service station open where I was able to get an overpriced two-prong wall plug. I wasn't able to charge my phone there but decided to do it later on. I had other things on my mind, crossing into the Czech Republic. There had been no border crossings up till now. One country blurred into another and as a foreigner you often don't even notice. Everything is still in Euros. You're still pointing at food you want to order and people can shout at you from their car windows in all sorts of languages and it all kind of sounds the same when you're as fatigued as I was. Crossing from Germany to the Czech Republic however was the start of the real challenge. Things would feel very different, the roads I presumed wouldn't be as good, different money and unfamiliar food all adding to the sense of real adventure. Life on the road was about to get a lot harder. It always takes a few days to get into the swing of things in a new country by which time I would have reached the Polish border and have to start all over again, learning new menus and new ways of asking for the Three C's without offending anyone. Pretending to squat on an invisible toilet was met with more suspicion the grubbier I was becoming.

My nervousness was tinted with a hit of sadness too. This would potentially be the point at which Pedro would no-doubt be forced to leave the adventure. I'm not sure what the rules are for taking a dead carcass across an international border, but I presumed it was in the 'Definitely not allowed' column. Considering you get fined $100 for taking an apple into Australia I was certain Pedro would be confiscated. This came with its own dilemma. I could leave him in a bush and sail through the border hassle free. This saddened me. The reason I brought him with me was to get him out of that bush he'd been in for a decade. I couldn't just leave him. If I tried to take him across I would no doubt have to deal with all the questions surrounding why on earth I had a dead dog's head strapped to the front of my bike. This would surely cost me a lot of time – time I couldn't afford to waste.

Eventually as the border approached I decided to chance it. I couldn't bear to leave Pedro in a bush. I took off my buff and covered him up.

My heart skipped a few beats when I saw the sign for the border just ahead. I guessed it would take me an hour to get through, or even longer if they found Pedro. The fact I had covered him up meant I was purposefully trying to smuggle something. I doubt Jonas had been in this same predicament. He seemed far more sensible than I was.

It was eerily quiet as I approached the border control. It was a few hundred meters ahead of me and I used this time to make sure Pedro was entirely covered. I checked, checked again, and rechecked to see that a tooth wasn't poking out. My heart raced and raced as I approached. There was no one around but it was 5am so wasn't expecting much activity. Eventually I came up to the first booth. It was empty. Suddenly a car drove past me and hooted as it sped off. I immediately thought sirens were going to go off. This chap had clearly jumped the border crossing. But nothing happened. Silence returned. Only the fluttering of my heartbeat. I continued past more official looking buildings until eventually I was past it all and reached a Czech Republic flag signpost. Was that the border? Was I in? I looked at my maps and it seemed I was in fact across the seemingly non-existent border.

I took the buff off Pedro and swore I saw him smile. If anyone stopped me now I would say I had just found him.

I was later to discover that The Czech Republic joined the Schengen Area in 2007 where all passport controls were taken away. 10 years it's been like this. My serious lack of planning skills rearing its ugly head again. All that wasted worry for nothing.

Now safely across the border I needed two things. Charge my phone and find an ATM to withdraw money. I managed to find another service station which had an adjoining café and was happy to realise Germany and The Czech Republic use the same wall plugs, something that had completely escaped me when buying the 30 Euro plug earlier. While my phone charged, I went back to inspect my dynamo. All the cables seemed to be in working order but it seemed intermittent when the battery bank was actually receiving power. To check this I would pick up my handle bars and then spin my wheel. While the wheel spun, which was only for about 10 seconds due to the drag from the dynamo, I'd have to move various cables around with my one free hand. 10

seconds was not nearly enough time before the wheel dropped below 5mph which was the minimum speed it needed to produce power. I just couldn't work it out. I wasted an hour in the café getting my phone charged until it reached 80% and I couldn't leave it any longer. I needed to get back on the road.

With my battery issues put aside I now needed to get money. Before that however I needed to know how much to withdraw. I tried to search online for the exchange rate but my GPRS signal wasn't strong enough for the internet. While in the café however, I noticed the cost of fuel to be 28CZK per litre. I figured that the price of fuel to be somewhere in the region of £1 per litre as it had been in some parts of Spain. I guessed it wasn't as expensive as Germany. So with that assumption, I rounded the number to an estimated 30 Czech Koruna to £1. I was spending on average £30-£50 per day on food so decided that I needed to draw 2,000 Koruna to cover me the 2 days it'd take to get across to Poland. I have used this system before and it's surprisingly accurate. It then came with great satisfaction to later discover the official exchange rate to be 29 to 1. I had been bang on. Feeling suitably smug and with a wallet full of interesting money and eastern Europe ahead of me, I soldiered on with an extra spring in my step.

The roads weren't as dramatically terrible as my mind had made them out to be. They, for the most part, were OK, except for the last metre on the edge of the road. This bit was almost always broken up which made things a lot slower. Cars weren't too bad either. The drivers seemed to drive a lot faster than the speed limit on the smaller roads but no close shaves, although my threshold for 'a close shave' is somewhat high nowadays. Even with the constant worry about being run over, you practically have to hit my elbow with your wing mirror (which has happened to me), and I'd still probably consider it a near miss.

'They can be as close as they want, as long as they see me,' I thought as I kept remembering Rory's saying that no one wants to run over a cyclist. Make it as easy as possible for them not to.

Being ahead of Jonas all day was a huge weight off my shoulders but I couldn't afford to slow down. Now was the time to keep or extend my lead. I pushed hard until midday when the hills started to appear. And were they tough. Like that second day in France it was 5 minutes up and 1 minute down all day on top of a cracking side wind that constantly blew me into the road. My pace was slow but I guessed Jonas would have been slow too.

The hills eventually started taking their toll on my energy levels. I hadn't had a good quality carb meal in days. Processed croissants and service station muffins just weren't good enough. I needed some good carbs, potato, rice or pasta. Pasta was the easiest to come by, but the problem with pasta is that it's hard to have it without actually going to a restaurant and ordering it, which takes too much time. I had been eating pot noodles and other 'add hot water' noodles straight out the bag, like you would crisps. This is surprisingly tasty but didn't meet my energy requirements as proper fresh pasta would.

With my mind now focused on getting a real pasta meal, I then wondered if I could eat raw pasta. This would save me at least half an hour. I figured it may soften in my stomach and then give me a slow source of energy. It was genius. So genius in fact that for the next hour, as I made my way to the next village, I had practically started my own raw pasta slow release energy company. I was going to take it to Dragon's Den and make millions. I couldn't wait to discover this new method of taking on calories. I couldn't believe no one had thought of it before.

I eventually found a supermarket and bought a bag of pasta. I decided on one of those bags that include the powdered flavouring. Not the pot noodle type, still proper pasta you need to cook. The powder just added a bit of flavour. These people were literally doing my job for me. I tore it open like a kid at Christmas and poured a few bits into my mouth and started chewing. Crack, crack, crack. Dammit, the pasta was rock hard. Who knew raw pasta was so solid? I persevered though, but it took me about 5 minutes just to get through a mouthful and I very nearly choked on a few larger pieces that got caught in my throat. That wasn't a great start to my business plan but I took solace in the fact it was cooking away in my belly doing its magic. I then decided on another idea. I could perhaps pour some water into the bag and let the pasta absorb it and get softer over the next few hours while I cycled along. Genius, I thought again and got my water bottle out and filled the bag as much as possible leaving enough room to fold the top over to avoid spillage. It was only after I finished pouring that I remembered I had some energy drink in the bottle from earlier on, Lucozade I think it was. Never mind. This was but a small hiccup in the flavour department but the theory would still work. I stuffed the packet into my back pocket, ate some pain au chocolat that I was going to save for dessert and continued west.

By early evening I was ready to eat my body-heated pasta which should be soft enough after stewing in my stinking back pocket for the best part of 4 hours. I wasn't expecting complete softness but soft enough to get down me without breaking a tooth. I opened the bag and put my hand in. Dammit. The pasta was still rock hard. Maybe the bottom bits had absorbed all the water. I dug further. Nope. The bottom bits were just as hard. This had not gone as I had expected at all. Disillusioned that my idea hadn't worked, I threw the pasta away and ate another disgusting processed croissant which too had been sweating away in my other back pocket. Some of the melted chocolate went deep into my beard where it remained for the next 3 days.

With my focus back in cycling mode, and not stupid food businesses, I searched for a suitable forest ahead. There was one 30 miles away and the perfect time to stop for the evening. I reached the sheltered woodland by 10.30pm and found a dense bit to camp up.

Soon after, I had stripped naked, rubbed a branch up and down my leg, waved at the potential CCTV camera in the trees and squirrelled into my sleeping bag. For the next 10 minutes I watched the moon rise through the trees. It was a beautiful night and I wanted to see a shooting star but fatigue soon took its grip and I fell asleep.

Getting support along the way

Race Time: 11 Days. 10 Hours. 13 Minutes
Location: Zdirec, Czech Republic
Miles Cycled: 1895

It started to rain again at 3.13am so I got up. This had not been in the forecast and to add insult to injury I could still see the moon and stars so it looked like one small rogue rain cloud had found me and decided I needed waking up. My camping mat too seemed to be leaking air faster than usual and I had to blow it up twice in the night. Immensely tired and somewhat grumpy, I packed up camp and was on the road by 3.32am.

My mood lifted slightly when I saw a deer prancing through the forest. It looked so graceful. I wanted to be that deer. Effortlessly gliding up the hill without even panting. I, on the other hand, felt like an old man who'd smoked 50 a day for his whole life as I huffed and puffed up the first hill while my legs took a while to realise they weren't asleep anymore, something that seemed to take longer and longer each day. The deer disappeared and I was left with nothing but my own thoughts which inevitably turned to my stupid charging issues. I needed to fix the problem as soon as possible. I still had another 2,100 miles to cycle and having to wait in cafés to charge my phone could cost me the record. In the dark it was easier to see when my battery bank was taking charge because the light went blue. This was hard to see in direct sunlight. I cycled along moving all the cables around to find the problem. I bent down and went to wiggle the cable down by the dynamo. Not concentrating my finger went right through the spokes and SMACK, the end of my fore-finger felt like it had been sliced off.

'Bollocks!' I shouted. Pedro laughed.

After shaking my hand around as if I was the world fastest guitar player, I then carefully put my hand down and wiggled the cable around again. It didn't seem to change anything. I then worked my way up moving all the different cables and where they connected to. The last one I checked was the cable connection into the battery bank. I moved this around and saw the blue light come on, then turn off. I moved the cable to the right and it turned on and to the left it turned off. Yes. So either the cable was dodgy or the port into the battery bank. I stopped and swapped out the micro-USB cable again. I carried on cycling and found the same thing happened with a new cable. When I pushed the cable over to the right it took charge and over to the left it didn't. Result. The issue was the port going into the battery bank. I stopped and got some insulation tape that I had wrapped around my water bottle. This is a good place to store tape you may need while bike packing, saves space in your bag. I moved the cable to the correct position and taped it. This worked perfectly and my battery bank was happily taking charge from my dynamo again. It was such a weight off my mind having power again. I worked out I had lost around 3 hours because of it.

My day got better when I found food early on even though I discovered whole hard bits of pasta in the toilet. Turns out that your body is not able to cook and digest raw pasta and therefore my business plan was a non-starter. I had truthfully kind of lost interest in the idea anyway. Pedro and I were already onto bigger and better ideas, but for the life of me I cannot recall any of them. I do remember the feeling I had when thinking about those ideas. I felt alive with excitement. Who knows, maybe one day they'll come back to me and I'll be able to change the world or something.

I was back in the café, ordering a much-needed coffee and getting my croissants when a homeless looking drunk fella came into the service station. It was 7am and he had a can of lager in his hand. I immediately looked at the service station attendant knowing full well she would tell him to go away. Instead she looked at him and a huge smile came over her face. She then shouted, whooped, put her arm in the air and called out a name that I guessed to be his. He then smiled back, put his beer in the air, gave a 'cheers', and then downed it. The girl behind the counter was then joined by another attendant and they both whooped and cheered at the chap. He finished his beer, crunched it, put it in the bin, went to the fridge, got another one and went to pay for it. They were all chatting away and seemed to love this old guy as he started swaying from side to side with extended periods of closed eyes. Then the music got louder. Heavy dance music, and they all started jigging and dancing on the spot. The 2 girls behind the counter and the drunk guy in the aisle. Was this really happening? It seemed this Shell Garage was the go-to-place after an all-night bender. I sat there for another 20 minutes while my phone charged still wondering if this was all happening. This service station was practically a nightclub, albeit with only 2 guests, and one of them was me. We both smelled though, so we had at least that in common.

I soon left the warmth of the service station nightclub and concentrated on the next milestone, the 2,000-mile mark. Today I'd reach the halfway point. This excited me as I only had 2,000 miles left, and also scared me because I thought about the last 12 days and what I had been through and the fact I'd have to do it all over again but this time in harder countries with worsening roads. Russia was still playing heavily on my mind and although I managed to keep it from affecting me, it was still there, gnawing away at my confidence, enticing my fatigued brain to think 'give up and go home.'

As the morning sun rose high in the sky the pollen count went through the roof. It was only this year that I have become somewhat lactose intolerant and with all the coffee and milkshakes I was drinking, my nose was constantly running which led it to bleed profusely. With the added pollen in the air I now had itchy eyes and was sneezing blood every few minutes. Luckily I had hay-fever tablets which was about the best forward thinking I've ever done. I may have forgotten a wall charger for my phone but at least I could stop sneezing on cue.

There is always something that annoys me each day. It's as if the cycling gods have a long list of things I need to overcome and as soon as I fix one of them, they send another one my way. As soon as I fixed my charging issue, all of a sudden my gloves wouldn't work on my phone screen anymore. I had the ones that are purposefully meant to work with phones and they had done brilliantly and without fail till now. It was too sunny to remove the gloves as I only just had enough sunscreen to cover my nose and cheeks each day. I didn't want to carry even more cream for my hands too. Normally I would cut the end of my gloves off, but I had no scissors. The only way to get the gloves to work was to put the finger tips in my mouth and soak the ends in spit. Once wet the phone screen recognised them and I was able to check my route. Now you have to remember my stinking gloves had been festering away on my hands for nearly 2,000 miles while getting all sorts of dirt, mud and roadkill flicked onto them from passing trucks. Putting my gloves in my mouth was undoubtedly one of the worst ideas I've ever had and would inevitably make me very ill. Looking back now I should have taken sun burn over getting ill, but at the time I thought it to be the better option. I could have just covered my hands in mud to protect them from the sun. I have done this before on my knees and calves once when I had run out of sunscreen and it works perfectly. How stupid I was to put those dirty fingertips in my mouth. Any illness would be the end of the record attempt.

The roads were much quieter and the side wind had died down which allowed me to keep a steady 12mph on the bike. The hills gave way for the flatlands and it became unbearably hot. I was drinking well over a litre an hour and using some of the 2 litres I was carrying to pour over my head and down my back to keep cool. It was no use, the hot side wind was like having a warm fan on me. I contemplated buying some frozen peas and putting them under my helmet but figured that was just another stupid idea.

The next thing on my to-do list was something I had been putting off since the start of the ride. Before I set off for Portugal I agreed to help with some of our wedding planning. Caroline didn't want me to do anything towards the wedding while I was away but I assured her it would be a good distraction from the pain and mundanity of spending 18 hours a day on the bike. This Europe record was slap bang in the middle of the most stressful part of our planning. We got engaged on a beach in Wales in February just 3 months earlier and were going to get married in July, two and a half months after I got back from Europe. We desperately wanted to have a Summer wedding and waiting till 2019 was not in line with an old British Gentleman's Quote I once heard.

'A proper British Gentleman should only be engaged for between 3 and 9 months whereupon he should then marry.'

I have no idea if this is true or not but we both liked the idea and planned to tie the knot less than 6 months after our engagement.

I can assure you it's quite hard planning a wedding in less than 6 months and Caroline was taking on a lot of responsibility while I was away. I still had a few things on my to-do list so for the next few hours real-life took over race-life as I searched for a suit for myself online which was surprisingly hard to do on the bike with gloves that didn't work. Thankfully the back roads were quiet. I called a few suit rental companies for my groomsmen's outfits, got a quote for the photography and most importantly chased up my uncle Gav on the huge pile of Biltong and Borewors we needed for our BBQ style wedding.

Time flew by and I very nearly missed the fact I was just about to reach 2,000 miles. It was 1,999 when I saw a WW2 bunker off to my right and decided that would be a good place to stop for my half way celebration. I had bought a beer a few hours earlier to have at this point. Even though it was warm it tasted fantastic as I mulled over the last 2,000 miles and read one of Caroline's letters which didn't bring me to tears this time. At 12 hours ahead of Jonas, I was feeling a lot more confident than I had done at mile 1,000.

With increased phone usage I was burning through my battery and went to charge it again from the battery bank and saw it wasn't taking charge. It looked like it hadn't taken charge all day as it was completely flat from when I had last used it to charge my phone overnight. I fiddled with the cable again and saw the blue light come on. It seems my taping hadn't quite kept it in the exact spot to take charge. I stopped and replaced the tape and added a few more loops around the cable to make sure it wouldn't move. This seemed to be a better job and the battery bank was taking charge again. The problem was that it was 8pm and with my phone practically dead, I now had no power. The only option was for me to check into a hotel and charge both my phone and battery bank to 100% overnight. This would also allow me to wash my clothes again. I was close to Poland so pushed on through to 9pm, crossed the non-existent border and made my way to the first hotel. Unfortunately it was full but the lady behind the counter seemed genuinely excited to practice her English with me which was a nice change from the rest of Western Europe that seemed less inclined to do so. She then proceeded to call a few hotels around but found them all to be full too. I said my thank yous and went back outside and called a few more that I found on Google. After the 4th one being full I resorted to calling some of the ones back in Czech Republic. I hated the idea of going back on myself but was desperate. Eventually I found one that was 6 miles back. That return trip plus all the hassle of calling around had cost me 2 hours. As it stood it took me 12 days to gain a 12-hour lead and in one evening I lost 2 days' worth of progress. But there was no point in getting stressed by it. I needed to charge my phone and that was that.

By midnight I had checked in, had one of the first sit down meals in weeks, another half pint and was tucked into bed in my wet clothes after washing them. I was half way, just another 2,000 miles to go.

2,000 mile mark

Race Time: 12 Days. 11 Hours. 45 Minutes
Location: Hat, Czech Republic
Miles Cycled: 2045

I treated myself to a lie in and got up at 5.45am. This was mainly due to Miss Moneypenny being locked in a garage and the hotel cleaner would only open it at 6am. So not only had I lost 2 hours last night I also was now getting on the road 2 hours later than normal. I did however have a good sleep, helped along nicely by the beer, no doubt.

By 6.30am I had crossed back into Poland and needed to get some money so stopped at the nearest ATM. I put my card in and various amounts of Polish Zloty came up on screen with the smallest option being 1,000 Zloty and the highest 4,000 Zloty. Normally in these situations I choose the second of the 4 options and guess it to be around £20. This I thought would be enough to at least get me through the day. I was just about to press the 2,000 Zloty button when something stopped me.

'Don't do it. Check the exchange rate first.' I didn't have the internet but remembered getting 3G just down the road so I cancelled the withdrawal and went to try and Google the official exchange rate. The first result that came up was that the Zloty was 20 to 1. That couldn't be right. At 20 to 1 the minimum to withdraw at that ATM was £50 and the maximum £200. It must be 200 to 1. I searched again and the same figure came up at 20 to 1. It couldn't be. After more searching and at least 10 minutes of my race time wasted it turned out the exchange rate was in fact 20 to 1 and I very nearly withdrew £100 for my 36 hours in Poland. I couldn't understand it at all but went back to the ATM, chose 'other amount' and withdrew 600 Zloty (£30) and continued.

Polish people, I think most would agree are considered very hard-working and this certainly showed through when I passed a chap walking in front of a van with a leaf blower. He was blowing the dust off a flyover. Yes, just dust. No leaves, no stones or debris, just dust. That, I can assure you, would be very hard work. With those sorts of jobs on offer no wonder they all flock to London to build immaculate houses for us.

I seemed to be getting a lot friendlier attention too as I cycled past people at bus stops. Smiles and head nods were becoming more common and this lifted my mood.

Diverting through the back streets down suburban lanes, showed off many of the big houses people seem to live in - some of those Polish builders making the most of their British Pounds - a sweeping statement I'll admit, but it must be true in some cases. It was eerily quiet again but I wasn't complaining as I got to explore the back lanes all to myself. This, I later I found out, was because it was Sunday and in Poland on Sunday you go to church. The few churches I passed were so full that people were standing outside listening to the sermon on loud speakers. The pride that they all put into the churches and graveyards was awe-inspiring. Most graveyards were so covered in flowers that you couldn't see the gravestones at all.

By lunchtime I felt a small rumble in my stomach and, convinced it was due to putting my infected gloves in my mouth, I decided to cut a hole at the end of my index finger. I didn't have scissors so decided to rub the end of the glove along the tarmac, using it like sandpaper. Annoyingly the gloves were a lot better made that I had expected and it took a good 10 minutes before I was able to rip a hole in the end and push my finger through. Conveniently, killing two birds with one stone, I also sanded down my fingernail which was getting quite long.

'Nail Clippers,' I suddenly shouted out loud.

It suddenly dawned on me that I did in fact have something to cut a hole in my gloves - nail clippers. It had totally slipped my mind. I could have cut them off yesterday avoiding having to put them in my mouth at all. I got them out from my bag and cut the rest of my nails and then while I was on the 'Nail clippers can cut anything' train of thought, I used them to trim the bottom of my moustache.

Being Sunday also meant the roadies were out. Fast chain gangs and club rides would bomb past me at lightning pace leaving me firmly in their dust, especially if Mr Dust Blower man hadn't been in town. Cycling in Poland is on the up and in 2014 they even boasted the road race world champion - Michał Kwiatkowski. Feeling pretty feeble with my ridiculously slow 15mph, which was only helped along by a little tailwind, I desperately tried to hang on the back of the third passing train of the day. I saw them coming in my mirrors and moved into big ring immediately. I gave it everything until I was bombing along at around 25mph, my legs burning and heart bouncing out of my chest, from exhaustion and excitement at the challenge. The 10 or so riders zoomed past saying something to me in Polish which I guessed to be 'Morning' or 'Is that really a dead dog on your handlebars?' I'll never know but they seemed in good spirits.

When the last guy passed I tucked in behind him and got launched forward by the back draft, pushing my pace up to 28mph. I pedalled like mad, teeth clenched to keep on, and it worked.

'We're doing it Pedro. We're on the train,' I shouted.

The chap ahead looked behind and laughed at me. Adrenalin pulsed through my veins. For the first time in a while I actually felt like a real cyclist. Like I was in the Tour de France, on the back of a raging peloton. Damn it felt good. I must have stayed on for about a minute, feeling on top of the world when all of a sudden I remembered something. Somewhere in the literature I had read before this record. It said something along the lines of: *No drafting allowed.*

'Bollocks,' I shouted again and the chap looked back at me with less excitement this time. Generally in big mile cycling, except the *'Most miles cycled in a year'* record, you are not allowed to draft. You usually have to have a 10 metre gap or cycle side by side if with another competitor in a race. My hanging onto the 'Sunday bullet train' was most definitely considered drafting. I stopped pedalling and within seconds was kicked out the back and saw the riders going off into the distance. They didn't even look back.

There and then I decided to give myself a time penalty. I came to a complete stop and stood there for 2 minutes not doing anything like, looking at my phone, drinking, eating, stretching or peeing. This was a proper time penalty and I shouldn't be doing anything that I may have stopped to do in 5 miles time anyway. 2 minutes was far beyond what I had gained from the minute on the train, but for my own peace of mind I felt it important to do so. The big mile cycling community is very much governed by honesty and integrity. Yes, I could have stayed on that train all day and no one would have known any different (until they read this book), just like I could hire a car to drive 12mph with my tracker on while I slept in the back and that too would undoubtedly go unnoticed but what's the point. Most big mile cyclists do what they do for no other reason than because they get personal satisfaction from it. And that's the exact reason I wanted to try and become a big mile cyclist. They're all just a solid bunch of people.

In good spirits the miles kept passing by as I rounded Krakov to the south. Afternoon lunch number 4 was a whole pizza freshly made which I wasn't charged for. Polish people were so far the friendliest I'd encountered on this ride and their enthusiasm to practice their English was infectious. I was slowly getting more confident about my Eastern European leg. Hopefully Russia would be the same.

By early evening, and having cycled 160 miles, I encountered another act of kindness. I was cycling along one of the main roads when I saw a chap with a huge red beard ahead of me waving and cheering. I smiled and waved back happy to find a fellow bearded chap, something I hadn't seen much of so far. It was only when I got closer that I saw he didn't actually have a beard at all. He had in fact cut out a piece of red paper in the shape of a beard and stuck it to his face somehow.

'Go Sean Go!' He shouted and cheered as I pulled up. He was a true gent and we chatted for a while about cycling and how he had come to meet Mark Beaumont on this exact road when he went around the world. He offered me some water which I didn't need but said thank you anyway and we cycled together for a few miles. He was on a mountain bike so the pace was slow but I didn't mind.

He eventually got back to his house and we parted ways. Poland was turning out to be my favourite country. It's a pity I'd be out the other side in less than 24 hours.

By nightfall, after having covered 175 miles, I found a field and wandered to the far corner to shelter under a tree. The forecast said it was due to rain at 4am but that was the time I was going to get up anyway so didn't bother too much. I did some stretching, tried to find a branch to roll my legs but couldn't so just punched my quads repeatedly until they were suitably tenderised. It had been a good start to the second half of the ride. I hoped it would continue.

It's calories, right

Race Time: 13 Days. 9 Hours. 55 Minutes
Location: Debica, Poland
Miles Cycled: 2220

It did not continue. As soon as I fell asleep I heard the unmistakable sound of a frisky stag just 100 metres from me. Its barks were so loud I thought at times he was about to bite my head off, or try and mate with me. At one point I got up and ran through the field completely naked towards the bark, shouting and screaming hoping that it would run away. It didn't. If anything, it seemed to make him more inquisitive. It was only at around 2am when he either found a girlfriend, or got bored, that he went away. At this exact moment however, the cycling gods throwing another challenge at me, a full moon rose bright above the horizon. The landscape turned to daylight and I was now completely visible from the road.

Not to mention the fact the moon was so bright I couldn't sleep either. Then just to add yet more insult, I felt a few drops of rain. Not enough to get me up but for the next 2 hours my mind was constantly worried about getting assaulted by a stag, seen by someone from the road or getting rained on. Eventually at 3.55am I got up as planned after having about an hour's sleep.

Bedraggled and weary beyond measure I started cycling again. It was Monday and the roads were sure to be a lot busier which I was not all too excited about either.

As always when I am tired, my mind plays tricks on me, so when a campervan driving in the opposite direction came to a screeching halt as I passed and then did a frantic U-turn to follow me I was convinced this was a repetition of the time when some gangsters were following me while I was cycling through the Atacama and I landed up getting a police escort. I was now being chased by a crazy man in a beat-up old camper van at 4.15am along a quiet back road in Poland.

Luckily today the cycling gods didn't want me dead and provided me with a service station 200 meters away. That was my safety. I sprinted hard and got there just before the camper. Safe in the knowledge there were CCTV cameras everywhere I left Miss Moneypenny outside and ran in. All the adrenalin meant I needed the loo desperately. A few minutes later I came out and saw the campervan was still outside. Inside the services was now a man, youngish, my age I guessed, just smiling and staring at me. He walked over slowly, said something in Polish and put his phone up to my face. My blurry eyes took a while to focus but I eventually saw a photo. It was of me with the guy who had the fake beard from

200

yesterday. We exchanged a few hand gestures as he couldn't speak English and we took another photo, said our goodbyes and he ran off back to his campervan. It was heart-warming to meet so many people in Poland who had seen something on Facebook or Instagram and made the effort to come and find me. I was just relishing these random acts of kindness, after having bought a coffee and some muffins, when the campervan chap came back and put the world's biggest cake in front of me. It was one of those prepacked cakes you buy in a supermarket but near on 1kg in weight, and smothered in various colours of icing sugar. As much as I knew I would later regret it, it was way too big to carry with me but didn't want to reject his kind offer. I said thank you and put it in front of me next to my coffee and waved him off into the darkness.

I really couldn't carry the cake but thankfully the service station sold the same ones so I just put it back on the shelf. I hated that a service station were the ones benefitting from his kindness but it was better than leaving it on the table and it probably landing up in the bin. 10 minutes later I was back on the road heading east towards Ukraine.

Various things scare me while on the bike. Not all the time, but every now and then I get reminded of the dangers of cycling on main or busy roads. Getting run over is the obvious one but there are others. Having a tyre burst on a fast descent. Cycling over a dog, rabbit or kangaroo crossing the road. The latter actually nearly happened to me when cycling across Australia. Snapping a front spoke at high speed. All these every now and then rear their ugly heads, especially when fatigued, giving me doubts and niggles about carrying on. Today something entirely new fogged my thoughts. Although I was on a main road, the road itself seemed to be going right through town after town. Houses that once were in sleepy suburbia now had a huge highway running through what would have been their back gardens. To avoid the residents going mad from the constant noise from passing trucks only 20 metres from their front doors, the highways agency had built 5 metre high sound barriers. You'll all have seen these before. Some are made from clear plastic, some of wood, but for the most part the ones in Poland were made of some sort of heavy duty slightly corrugated Styrofoam. They are obviously great at absorbing the road sound but what also happens is that they allow rocks that get flung from passing trucks to stay embedded in the foam walls. This over time gives a stark reality of just how many rocks get flung up and just how big these rocks are. Hundreds of golf ball sized rocks were lodged at exactly head height as I cycled past miles and miles of these sound barriers. Each rock sending chills down my spine. If one of those were to hit me, that would certainly be the end of my race, or even worse, potential death or serious brain injury. To make things worse I stopped to press the sound barrier foam to see if it hopefully was not as strong as the foam in my helmet. This would have given me some hope that maybe my helmet would save me, but disappointingly the sound barrier foam was almost as hard as cement to the touch, far stronger than the inside of my helmet. It was certainly a nerve-racking day every time a truck sped past me, constantly waiting for that fatal blow to the temple.

Along with the overwhelming worry about getting stoned, I was also properly worried about the Poland/Ukraine border crossing. This one I knew for sure was a real, proper, state of the art, angry faced guards with guns, don't look at me in that tone of voice, type of border. One that Pedro would almost certainly not make it through, and I feared would also land me at the wrong end of some rubber gloves if we got caught.

Land border crossings on a bike are always a bit tedious. Sometimes you're funnelled through with the cars. This is often much slower because the queues can be long. In the past when the queues have been longer than about 10 cars or more, and its pouring with rain for example, I have cycled to the front, put on a look of desperation and a huge smile hoping the driver in front will let me in. This often works. Not always though, and on one occasion I was nearly run over when a cycle-hating driver thought it completely illogical and unfair that I should be allowed to jump the queue. The reason I do often at least go to the front of the queue is that sometimes bicycles have to go with the foot passengers. I learned this the hard way on the Malaysia/Thailand land border when I queued politely for an hour with the cars and motorbikes only to be turned away to join the back of the long pedestrian queue in the end.

The queue of cars started miles from the border, and it looked like they had been there a while. People in campervans had their deck chairs out, beer and vodka bottles strewn everywhere. This looked like it was going to take me a while to get through. I pulled over to the side of the road and foraged for my nail clippers to cut the cable ties holding Pedro to my bars.

'Sorry buddy. It's time you stayed here for a while. It's probably more exciting for you,' I said out loud. I looked around for a bush to put him in. Annoyingly it seemed my nail clippers had fallen out the zip lock and were now either at the bottom of my bag or I had lost them altogether.

'It's a sign Pedro,' I said looking at his sad face. I felt sad too.

'Right. We're going to try and risk it again. I'll cover you up and hope for the best.'

I unwrapped the buff from the elbow pads on the aero bars and covered Pedro up. Nervous excitement started to build. I kind of liked it.

Feeling rebellious because I was now going to try and properly smuggle part of a dead animal carcass across an armed border, I figured there was no way I was going to wait in this queue, so I cycled past everyone right to the front. I eventually came to a closed gate where no cars were being let through. A few hundred metres past the gates were the toll booth style border guard huts but they were all empty. There were no cars, no people, nothing. The crossing looked like it had just decided to shut up shop and they weren't letting anyone through. By the looks of things at the front of the queue where everyone was out of their cars having a drink, this seemed to have been like this for a while. I got off Miss Moneypenny and put her on the floor and stretched my legs. Suddenly there was a huge arm wrapped around my shoulders. I panicked thinking I was being detained, but then I smelled it. The heavy stench of Vodka. I turned around to see the huge smile and cross-eyes of a large fellow, in a tank top, shouting, 'Photo, photo.' He spun me around and his mate, equally bleary-eyed, was trying to work out how to get his phone off selfie mode to get a picture with me. I just went with it. They weren't threatening at all. The big armed chap then let me go and proceeded to pretend he was a cyclist using his arms like legs running around in front of the row of cars. Everyone was jeering and laughing. I had to laugh too, it was rather funny. Then he stopped suddenly and pointed at me and pointed to a building on the other side of the fence to our left. He then suggested in a strangely coherent manner, using sign language, that it seemed I was to go with all the pedestrians in that building. I gesticulated back asking if I was to go there and they all said 'Da' in unison. He then ran over to a large plastic traffic bollard and kicked it so that it made a gap large enough for me to cycle through. I picked up Miss Moneypenny, said thank you and cycled off to, what I presume, were the well-wishes from my new drunken friends.

The pedestrian queue was not nearly as long as I had thought and I reached the first window within 10 minutes. I handed over my passport and had removed my helmet to show my full face, eager to please to avoid suspicion. The elderly, very stern looking woman in scary uniform looked at me, then looked at my passport, looked at me again, then stood up and leaned over to get a better look. She did this for a lot longer than I felt comfortable, convinced she had glimpsed Pedro under my buff. Then suddenly she said.

'OK. Go,' and pointed me to another window.

The same thing happened there but after a while they eventually said the same.

'OK. Go.' But this time I swore they pointed me to the door. I smiled, put my passport into the bottom of my tights and hurried for the door.

'Yes,' I thought. I'm through.

'Pedro we made it,' I said under my breath.

I couldn't have gone more than a metre when I heard a loud deep shout from another booth on the other side of the corridor from the first two. Everyone jumped. I looked around and saw another scary man glaring at me as if I was attempting to enter the Ukraine illegally.

'Passport!' he boomed. Everyone jumped again.

I took it out, slightly covered in sweat from being in my tights and handed it over. He was not impressed. He scrupulously went through every page as one would do to anyone who seemed like they wanted to hurry through passport control because they may have a dead dog in their possessions. This was it I thought. I had blown it. In my haste to get through, I appeared to be guilty of something and it seemed this angry Brian Blessed lookalike was going to have to rubber glove me. I contemplated trying to say something like; 'Wow I can't wait to visit Ukraine and spend loads of money to help your country's economy' but I figured he'd see right through my lies. I decided to just keep quiet and smile. The man did not smile back but eventually after looking at every page of my passport he gave it back and gave me a head nod towards the door. Passport back in tights I clobbered out on the slippery floor. Pedro and I had made it into the Ukraine, buttocks still intact.

As in the Czech Republic and Poland, I had the task of getting money. At the border were loads of places to exchange money but no ATM. The nearest was an hour away. I had completely run out of water an hour before the border and in my nervousness to get through hadn't thought to buy any, thinking I should be able to get some on the other side. An hour to ride with no water wasn't ideal but certainly not a disaster by any means. I had increased my lead to around 15 hours on Jonas now.

The first thing I noticed were the incredible churches in Ukraine. Gold roofed cathedrals dotted each town overlooking manicured paved gardens. Sadly I would not be in the Ukraine on the weekend to see them in all their glory. If their attendance was anything like Poland I can only imagine what a spectacle it would be. I'd just have to come back and visit again in the future, something I say a lot when doing these cycling records but it doesn't bother me. Big mile cyclists often get asked if they regret zooming through countries as if between traffic lights. They always answer no. They all have different reasons, Mike Hall's being that he preferred racing to sightseeing. I can totally relate to that. I'm not a very good traveller and sightseer. I get itchy feet unless I have a goal within my travelling and more often than not the goal has to be a physical challenge. I feel I get a lot more out of my wanderings this way. It's a bit like wine tasting. If you get a real nice glass you don't decide to stop the wine tasting session and refuse the rest of the wine that's on offer. You enjoy that small glass and the following 5, and go home happy that one day you may buy a bottle of the good one. It's the same for me when cycle touring. I enjoy brief encounters and 'fly on the wall' observations and know that one day I shall come back, hopefully with my wife and kids. That excites me a lot.

The second thing I noticed was the sudden increase in moustaches. Literally everywhere. This, not surprisingly, made me feel right at home.

Not falling for the same old cash machine trick, I worked out roughly what I needed and soon had a wallet full of interesting money again.

My first goal for the day was to get through L'viv. This would potentially be the biggest city I'd have had to cycle through so far and it looked like I was going to have to go directly through the centre of it. This seemed the best option because going around would add far too many miles.

I reached L'viv early evening and my pace dropped significantly. The first annoyance was that the traffic was terrible, at a standstill most of the time with not enough space to squeeze between cars. The second, and even more annoyingly, was that the entire town was cobbled. Bone wrenching, gut churning, neck breaking cobbles. At least I had the comfort of a steel bike but even so, it was tough to navigate. Running within the cobbles were tram lines too which, as many of you will have learned the hard way, if you get your wheel stuck inside one of the grooves, it's pretty much game over. It's your face, on the cobbles, before you've even realised your mistake.

The progress was painstakingly slow and it took me nearly 2 hours to get through to the other side. I found a service station to get food, which annoyed me no end because I had seen countless perfect places selling fresh pizza, pasta and burgers in the centre of L'viv but there was no place to leave Miss Moneypenny safely. I didn't have a lock and daren't leave her on the busy street while I ate inside. Most service stations at least had CCTV cameras.

Annoyed that I missed a good meal, I bought a packet of small croissants, a large bag of crisps and more water.

I had finished my food in a record 12 minutes and was just getting back on the road when a huge crack of lightning struck nearby. I nearly fell over. I could swear I heard Pedro howl. Seconds later the heavens opened. This was not forecast at all. I turned around and went back to the shelter of the service station. Now I know it seems whimpish to not want to cycle in the rain but I had a fairly good reason which was that it was nearly dark, which would make being seen on the road more difficult. Cars didn't seem to have the same rigorous safety testing as they would in the UK and seeing a car with an almost entirely cracked front windscreen was not uncommon. Broken windscreens, dodgy wipers and candle bright headlights was a certain recipe for an accident waiting to happen.

It would also make it harder to spot potholes in the puddles and breaking a spoke or damaging a rim would be the end of my record this far in. But the main issue was that if I got soaking wet now, I was too close to camping up for the evening to dry out and would have to get into my sleeping bag completely soaking wet which would result in my bag being wet and me being cold. I knew these sorts of thunder showers would pass quickly so sat down next to another commuter cyclist and a motor-biker, both of whom, had decided on the same idea.

While sitting on the edge of the pavement waiting out the storm, a man drove into the service station and filled his car up with fuel. He then went to the back of his car, opened the boot and began the laborious task of trying to remove a huge 42" TV still in its box. Eventually he got it out and carried it into the service station. None of this really got my attention until I then saw the man sitting with a cup of coffee in the cafe with the TV next to him. He was there for maybe 10 minutes before he got up, carried his TV back to his car, spent another age trying to fit it back into the boot and then drove off again. It seemed that he may have just taken his TV out for coffee. A date perhaps. Very strange I thought. Very strange.

10 minutes later the storm passed and I continued east, happy in the knowledge I would have a dry night ahead of me.

By 10pm it was time to find a place to camp. There had been fields of rapeseed everywhere and I decided that they would be the perfect place to rest up for the night, in amongst the rows and furrows, hidden from sight. I found a tiny access road up to a well grown field and cycled up it. The road was so overgrown I soon had to get off and push my bike through the long grass. This gave me a sense of security knowing that no one was going to come down the road in the night so I could sleep fairly close to it.

I nestled my way down one of the furrows and set up camp. The rapeseed was so dense that I only needed to go in about 2 metres and I was completely hidden. It was extremely cosy and the overhanging rapeseed stalks acted as a makeshift shelter to keep the dew off me. This was by far the best camp spot I had found since Portugal.

Amazing buildings in the Ukraine

Race Time: 14 Days. 9 Hours. 9 Minutes
Location: Busk, Ukraine
Miles Cycled: 2383

My alarm went off at 4am but I only managed to get out the sleeping bag at 9 minutes past. Even though I had slept well I was finding it harder and harder to get up each morning, my body trying everything in its power to convince me I needed more recovery time, and it was right. The restless sleep on the side of highways was taking its toll on my long-term fatigue. I was knackered and my camping mat still had a hole which meant blowing it up twice during the night, and one of those times I disturbed a rat that was wondering why a human was sleeping on top of his den. As fatigued as I was I still constantly worried about oversleeping. I was 15 hours ahead of Jonas and that had taken me nearly 15 days to achieve. If left alone I would easily oversleep by 5 hours or more, which would take me a week to claw back.

The first thing I do each morning when I wake up is open the air vent on the mattress. I do this while still lying down. My body then helps to expel the air more rapidly, saving me a few minutes on having to squeeze it out with my knees later. This morning was no different and I was just starting to feel the cold floor seeping through to my hips when all of a sudden a light shone through the rapeseed. My immediate thoughts were that it was someone with a torch coming to look for me. I still had my earplugs in so took them out. It wasn't a torch, it was a car, driving up the small side overgrown back road, that no one had driven down in years. How was this possible? I held my breath and just lay there. Millions of imaginary, and on reflection, wholly unrealistic, scenarios clouded my mind. Had I turned my tracker off? Something I normally did a few miles before camping each night so that people didn't know where I was sleeping. Had the farmer seen me creep into his field and was now coming to find me? The car crept forward and drove right up next to me. It was about 2 metres away, the engine still running. I peered up to see what type of car it was thinking that the type of car would possibly give me a clue as to the type of person driving it. I put my head up slowly and peered above the rapeseed. Damnit. It was a dodgy banged up saloon. Why was he here? This kind of behaviour I thought was akin to that of someone coming to dump a body. 4am. Small unused farm track. Dense rapeseed field. It was ideal for such an activity. I needed to get out of there. Luckily the rapeseed was high enough for me to stand Miss Moneypenny up and still be lower than the top. I got up slowly, and began to drape everything all over her frame and saddle like the world's worst washing line. 'How was I such a messy camper?' I thought to myself. Somehow one of my gloves was down the bottom of my sleeping bag and the other was in the next furrow on from where I was sleeping.

Then, and still completely naked, I kept my head hung low and tried to be as quiet as possible as I skulked past the car, my one saving grace being that the engine was still running which dampened out the sound of my rear wheel hub clicking away. I still wasn't 100% sure the driver, now an axe wielding murderer, hadn't got out the car but that didn't matter. I just needed to get back down to the main road. When I was behind the car I then stood up straight and sprinted as fast as I could, which proved to be harder than I expected while pushing a mobile clothes horse.

As luck would have it, I reached the main road as soon as an elderly couple were driving past. I was a deer caught in the headlights, stark bollock naked, with a bike laden in stinky clothes, looking terrified on the side of the road.

'Don't stop. Please don't stop,' I said out loud. Luckily I looked more like someone to avoid than to help and the car sped past me, noticeably swerving and accelerating away. I then ran over the road to the opposite side, found a bush and got changed. It was a miracle that I came out with all my possessions. The only thing I lost was my dignity, and that I can live with. I can only apologise to the unassuming couple who will probably repeat this story for years to come. The time a crazy, hairy, skinny ginger chap ran out of a rapeseed field completely naked at 4.20am.

To add salt to my wound, about 1 mile from the rapeseed field were 2 pristine, comfortable, rat-free, murderer-free hotels. It was that time of the week again where I could have done with washing my clothes. My saddle sores were getting progressively worse and the slight spray from yesterday's rain had made all the salt in my shirt run down into my crotch, literally adding salt to the wound this time. I also realised that I hadn't just lost my dignity on the side of the road. I had lost my sunglasses too. This had not been a good start to the day. The only positive thing that came from the morning was that I didn't have a headwind. I didn't have a tailwind either, but at least I could keep a good 15mph.

The roads in the Ukraine continued to be good. Mostly flat with a nice hard shoulder in places. I knew my fatigue was getting worse when at around midday I thought I saw a fluffy ginger and white guinea pig dash across the road in front of me. It's extremely common to hallucinate during these big mile records and I knew that if that started to happen I needed to get some rest. I desperately needed a night in a hotel.

Even though I was keeping my head down all day, rural Ukraine was a pleasure to cycle through. Old aged husband and wife teams ploughing fields and planting seeds, friendly faces whenever someone looked up to see me and the occasional friendly hoot from passing cars made the miles fly by. The only one further annoyance, after nearly getting murdered of course, was that I got overtaken by another cyclist on a fixie. He bombed past me on a slight incline. I tried to catch up but my legs said no. This confirmed the fact that I was now in deep, long-term fatigue, which I would not get over till the end. It would be a case of survival now. Keep my 15-hour lead and play it safe. That's the only strategy possible. My attack days were long behind me now.

Even in survival mode I had done 170 miles by 6pm. I think the adrenalin from the morning's wake-up call certainly helped. It was around now that I needed to look for a hotel for a good rest and to clean my clothes. There were two places ahead. One 10 miles away and another 18 miles away. That was a tough call. Ideally I would go ahead to the 18 mile hotel as that was a better place to stop but I'd hate to skip the first one and the second one be fully booked. I decided to play it by ear, but truthfully, I had already decided to play it safe and take the first stop I could find. A shorter day with a good bed and clean clothes was more important.

An hour later I arrived at the first hotel. It was incredible. Fairly new, built with love and care out of brown stone. There were balconies coming off every room and an outside decking area where a few people were smoking and drinking and laughing. The carpark was filled with trucks and it seemed a popular place for truckers to get a night's rest. I wheeled Miss Moneypenny up the stairs and to the front door. Inside, the lighting was warm and friendly and the décor to match any hotel around London. It was perfect. All ideas to push ahead were completely buried so far to the back of my mind, it was hard to imagine I ever had them. I was dreaming about a warm bath as I made my way up to the reception desk.

'Hallo,' I said not knowing why I added the 'a' to hello. Sounded more foreign I guess.

The guy just looked up at me.

'Do you have a room available?' I asked excitedly.

'No,' he said and looked back down at his computer.

'Really? Nothing at all. Not even a family room?'

'No. Sorry. For truck only,' he said seemingly less annoyed now, possibly taking the pleasure in refusing a smelly cyclist a room.

'Oh. This hotel is only for truck drivers?'

'Yes.'

'There is no way I can stay?'

'No. Not possible.'

'OK. Is there anywhere else to stay around here?'

'10km that way,' he said and pointed back up the road the way I had come.

'OK,' I just said and sulked my way out.

This was not good and also, how had I missed the hotel from 10km back? It looks like I was going to land up in the next hotel. At least I'd get a few more miles in.

I reached the next place where Google said there was a hotel and it looked far more promising. A roadside arcade type place with stalls and games. I asked around for a hotel and they pointed me down an alley. I went down and saw nothing. I went and asked someone else. They too pointed me down this ally. I went again in case I had missed it but again it was nothing but a car park at the end, and empty car park at that.

I tried this three more times and eventually decided that maybe they all misunderstood me and I was wasting too much time. I had lost at least half an hour already. I got back on my bike and carried on cycling, hoping that I may find a hotel that wasn't on Google a few miles away. I continued till I reached 193 miles for the day and decided that I just needed to give up on the hotel idea. You win some, you lose some and today I lost. At least I had cycled a big day and that made up for it. I had contemplated sleeping in a bus shelter but the few I went into stank of pee and were quite open fronted. It would be easy for passing cars and murderers to see me. The other place I looked into were the toilets that were just behind each bus stop. Public loos can be a great place to crash. You can usually curl up somewhere away from the loo itself, near the hand dryer or something. Sadly Ukrainian bus stop loos were just long drops, and pretty disgusting ones at that. In fact the loos were so awful that I had to dodge about 50 turds on my way to the loo. I still can't tell you why I even bothered carrying on to check the loo itself but I did and nearly threw up in my mouth.

I eventually found a bush just near the road and settled in. There had been some mosquitos around earlier in the evening but they seemed to have disappeared. It had been an interesting day and even though I hadn't managed to find a hotel, I felt good in the knowledge that I hadn't been murdered.

Race Time: 15 Days. 9 Hours. 20 Minutes
Location: Zhytomyr, Ukraine
Miles Cycled: 2573

It seems my sleeping bag has lost all ability to breathe. The salt from my sweaty body was now hard-packed into the fabric of the inside of the bag. It smelled pretty disgusting too. Because it doesn't breathe it means that it basically becomes a microwave in the night and I sweat even more and it becomes a downhill spiral. This is because my sleeping bag had no zip. This was a weight saving design. But it means I can't unzip it if I'm too hot to let some heat out. Then, because I am soaking wet, when the temperature does cool at around 3am I get freezing cold. All in all, getting a good night's sleep on the side of the road was becoming near on impossible. What I really need to do is take my clothes off and stand around in the forest cooling off before getting in the bag. I did this at the beginning when I was rubbing sticks on my thighs and, on reflection, those nights were pretty comfortable. I think I may have to revisit my hidden bird watching camera dance moves.

I would however have to wait to test this out till tomorrow night because I despairingly needed a hotel where I could wash my clothes tonight.

Today was a significant day too because I had now exactly 10 days of cycling to get to Ufa in order to get the record. Quick calculations suggested about 1,430 miles to go but it could be around 1,500. This was good news. 150 miles per day seemed not just achievable, but almost easy. 150 miles per day on Russian roads however, may be a little tougher, but still, I was feeling confident.

The morning continued as every other morning. Finding food, keeping my head down and an average pace covering 12 miles per hour including stops. It was around 11.30am when I looked in my mirrors and saw a 'proper' cyclist coming up behind me in the distance. I could tell he was on a 'real' bike as opposed to a casual town bike that I had seen mostly so far. The rider's position was slightly more hunched forward. It had straight bars and looked kind of like a hybrid bike with two panniers on the back.

'Another tourer Pedro,' I shouted in genuine excitement to have a cycling buddy. When I cycled around the world I met Polish Paul in Croatia and we had a great 3 days cycling together. By then I wasn't racing anymore so we both were doing short 130-mile days. I doubt this chap behind me wanted to do long days but I would potentially have someone to cycle with for today, and that excited me.

I slowed down and a few minutes later he came to within 10 metres of me and then slowed too. I looked in my mirror. He was a young chap. Late 20's perhaps, wearing lycra, clip in shoes, and listening to music. He looked tough, his expressionless face determined to achieve something. I wondered what? He cycled behind me for twenty minutes, obviously not as excited about cycling with someone as I was, and whenever I turned around he barely acknowledged me. He did nod his head slightly but I wasn't sure if that was because of the music he was listening too. A far cry from Enya who had shuffled her way into my headphone.

He didn't look Eastern European either and then suddenly a terrible thought crossed my mind. What if this chap was also going for the Europe record? It would have been a genius tactic. I made such a song and dance before the start, anyone would have known my departure date. Yes, I delayed my announcement till as late as possible but after my last failed attempt it wasn't rocket science to work out that I was going to have another crack at it. What this chap had done, and it's what I would have done too, is start his attempt one day after me. All he would have needed to do was catch me, which at a rough estimate would have taken him till about today, and then he'd just need to match my pace. He could literally tail me all the way to the end and beat me by one day. Bollocks it was a good plan. Everything about his set up and the way he was cycling suggested he could have done this. My heart sank. There was no way I could claw back a day on him, providing he started a day after me. It could have been 2 days, but probably not 3.

The conditions weren't good enough to pull 3 days on me, possibly not even 2 really. Either way this was not ideal. How had I let this guy slip through the net? I had researched high and low for my competition and Leigh Timmis seemed to be the only one.

I stepped up a gear to try and pull away from him but he stepped up too and stayed 10 metres behind me, the distance you have to stay to avoid drafting rules. He was now my enemy and I needed to get away from him. I couldn't lose this record now. I pushed hard again and started up a small climb. I should have dropped down a gear but I didn't and pushed even harder. That's when I heard it go. 'Twing!' I felt a sharp pulse run up my right VMO, the inside quad muscle. I eased off. Sensing my change in pace I saw him get out the saddle and pushed past. He flew by as if I was going backwards and didn't even turn to nod, or say hi. Deflated, I came to a slow halt as he disappeared over the next crest.

I rubbed my VMO to warm it up. It wasn't a pull, not like last year. It seemed just a slight twinge. I stretched it out and continued, slowly. My pace dropped about a mile an hour, which would add an hour to my day, meaning I'd either lose an hour's sleep, or mean I'd be 10-15 miles short of my daily target. I limped on slowly to the next service station and sat down for food and a coffee. For half an hour I searched the internet for anyone else who was potentially going for the Europe World Record. Nothing came up. No-one except Leigh and his supported ride in a few months' time. This didn't help me though. If someone had all the funding already and didn't need sponsors, all they would do is turn their tracker on and start riding. It wouldn't be online or social media at all. There was obviously still a huge chance that he was just a commuter or going for a weekend ride, in the week, but I couldn't help but think the worst. Sleep deprivation giving me heightened paranoia.

Kiev was next on my horizon. I knew it would be slow to get through but took solace that both Jonas, and Johan (the name I gave to my new challenger) would have taken time to get through too.

Kiev was slow and dangerous at times as I found my way onto a fast dual carriageway with no hard shoulder. It had a sold brick wall just centimetres from my bars to my right, and cars passing me centimetres from my bars to my left. I was sandwiched between fast cars and a brick wall and the road was so busy I couldn't find a gap to get across to the safety of the pavement on the other side. The only way to make cars give me a wider birth was to do a fake wiggle as if I was unsteady on the bike. This tactic really does work and cars will move over. I have even given it a name. I call it The Bradley Wiggle.

I struggled on but my sense of humour finally failed when I got lost and landed up on a long cobbled downhill, heading back towards Portugal. It was so bumpy and slippery I had to get off and walk for fear of slipping and going head first under a lorry. Kiev was not playing ball, but determined not to lose any more time, I forwent my food stop and pushed on.

By mid-afternoon the toll of my pulled VMO and the slow route through Kiev started to show in my dismal mileage. It had taken me 12 hours to do 120 miles. The 150 miles per day target that I had thought to be easy was turning out to be not so. Then at mile 135 Ukraine decided to add yet another peril in the shape of a wolf. It wasn't alive; it was dead, a bit of roadkill. Having grown up amongst wild animals in Africa I've learned a few things about animal behaviour. It's not the Lion that you stumble across while walking in the middle of the bush that is the biggest worry, it's the old, scraggly, starving one that is so desperate for food it needs to come to urban areas to scavenge. They are the dangerous ones. Seeing remains of a wolf on the side of the road suggested an old wolf looking for food and what better meal than a smelly, lean cyclist half roasted already in a sweaty sleeping bag camping right next to the road. I really did need a hotel.

My saddle sores were getting worse too. It seemed everything was out to stop me today. Determined to carry on I did so, but only for another hour when I passed the only sign for a hotel I had seen all day. It was too much to pass on. I had only done a dismal 148 miles.

Although it said Hotel on the outside I couldn't for the life of me find it. All there seemed to be were soviet style concrete apartment blocks with small windows and heavy iron doors. Where was this hotel? I walked back and forth until I saw someone and asked him. He pointed at one of the iron doors. It seemed unlikely and it's possible there was a communication problem but I went and rang the dodgy intercom because he was watching and I didn't want to be rude. I waited a bit and was about to give up when I heard a woman's voice on the line.

'Hello. You have room?' I said in the patronising traveller way and hated myself for it. I heard the buzzer. I pushed the heavy door open and went inside. The short corridor was dark and damp but lead to a small flight of stairs and to another glass door. When I entered my jaw literally dropped. I was fully expecting a dilapidated, cockroach infested, dimly lit motel. This was far from it. In fact, it could easily have passed as a mid-range fancy hotel in London where there is no reception and someone accosts you with an iPad to check you in. Such a strange juxtaposition between feeling like you're about to go into a crack den and landing up in a day spa.

It took half an hour of Google translate to check in and find a place to store Miss Moneypenny so that I could leave at 5am the next day. I then went straight for the shower and spent another half hour rinsing and washing my clothes with the free shampoo. Annoyingly, this was one of those hotels that give you the shampoo sachets, rather than the larger miniature bottles. Nevertheless, it was quite disgusting what had collected in the shower bowl.

After the shower, I was back in my room doing some stretches when I felt something on the back part of my hip. It felt like a spot or saddle sore. Possibly from the salt build up. I tried to squeeze it in case it was full of puss but instead it felt like a little hard bit that was flacking off the skin. I pulled and my skin lifted. I turned to look and to my horror saw that it was a tick. I pulled it off and a bit of my skin went with it. If you have one tick, you often have more. This was true, as I found another on the other side of my hip, right at the place where my tights ended, a perfect snug spot to drink my blood. Now I've been bitten by ticks a lot, more times than I can guess, with my record being 38 in one day. But those ticks didn't have the one thing I was now dreading – Lyme Disease, something that Ukrainian deer ticks most definitely have.

So all in all, today had not been a good day. For every day I do less than 150 miles, it adds more pressure to the final Russian leg. I felt like the last week I was just scraping by. I needed to just get my act together, one or two more attack days is what I really needed, but I just couldn't see any way of making that happen. I was just too fatigued. I desperately wanted to feel in control of my race again. Feel and know my limits and push as close to them as humanly possible. But as I sat there on my bed, short of mileage, a torn VMO, terrible saddle sores and with potential Lyme Disease, I felt for the first time a sense that I may still lose this record at the last hurdle.

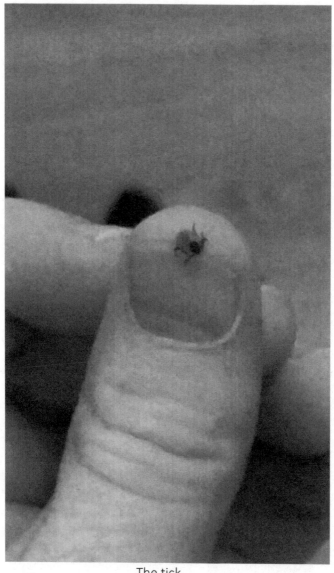

The tick

Race Time: 16 Days. 10 Hours. 0 Minutes
Location: Kozelets, Ukraine
Miles Cycled: 2721

Up at 5am again and this time my hips hurt near the tick bites. I know that this is partly psychosomatic, but none the less I couldn't help but think about the possibility of Lyme Disease. At least my clothes, which I had worn overnight, were nice and dry and salt free, which made the morning session a bit more bearable.

The pain in my arse thankfully disappeared a few hours in when I saw a dead guinea pig on the side of the road, which meant I wasn't going mad when I saw one the other night. At least my sanity was still intact it seemed.

The east part of Ukraine was long straight and flat, something my VMO very much needed. Had I got this niggle in the hilly sections of France I think it may have ended my attempt. On the flats, however, I could use my hamstrings to keep a reasonable average pace. The downside with these long straight roads was that they were terribly boring and I found it hard to keep a positive mindset. I was convinced that the only thing keeping me from actual madness, was the fact that this evening I was going to cross into Russia. Normally there is a mixture of nervousness and excitement when going somewhere new but I can tell you, the Russian leg for me was all nerves. There was no excitement at all. I had not built up enough of a lead to take it easy in Russia. I was now roughly 26 hours ahead of Jonas but with 1,200 miles of terrible roads, a notoriously relaxed drink driving culture, a right leg working at 50% and what was looking like a constant a headwind, there was still a chance I may not break the record.

I was also going to do a different route to Jonas on the Russian leg. He went on a north road and his Instagram suggested it was a terrible route with huge trucks passing inches from his head. There was a southern route which was about 30 miles shorter on a bigger highway. The thinking was that hopefully bigger roads would have a larger hard shoulder. The downside was that to get to this southern route I was going to cross into Russia at a border crossing that could very well be shut. It was on a real tiny back road, but I had to risk it. Going to the northerly border crossing first was too far off course.

It was 6pm when I finally turned off the long straight main road and then onto a dirt track. This was not a good sign. It would be 2 hours before I would get to the border and if it was closed it would be 2 hours back again and then possibly 3 hours to go north, around the top and back down to my southern route. So today I could potentially lose 7 hours to Jonas and who knows where Johan was. But if it worked I'd gain nearly 3 hours.

My average dropped to around 8 miles per hour to avoid getting a puncture. It was getting dark too and I again decided to skip my evening meal just to get to the border.

By 8pm I could see the lights of the border ahead. It looked open. I came around the last corner before the long double barbed wire fence started running along the road. This was by far the most serious border crossing I'd ever been to. 30 metres further on and 3 armed guards came into view, all walking in a line towards me, machine guns casually hanging from their shoulders, and not in their hands, which would have been a lot more intimidating. I smiled when I cycled passed them and they cheered at me and said something I didn't understand. I waved and said hello. At least they were in a good mood. Things were looking up.

I reached the first gate and was asked for my passport from another stern looking man with a gun. He looked at it briefly and pointed me to a cabin 50 metres away. I went there and another stern gentleman, without a gun, sent me to another window. In there was the scariest of them all. A young skinhead, with facial scars one only gets from wars or bar fights. He looked at me, then at my documents.

'Ukraine?' he said asking me if I spoke Ukrainian?

'No, sorry. Only English,' I replied. He looked annoyed.

'Russia?'

'No, Sorry,' I said again even more apologetically.

'Come,' he said and started walking to a metal platform. I followed.

'Put,' he said again asking me to put Miss Moneypenny up against the railing.

'Where you cycle?'

'Portugal to Russia for Guinness.'

'Guinness?' He replied looking somewhat impressed even though his facial impression suggested he wanted to bury me alive.

He then shouted over to another guard who came over. He then said something to him and I heard the word Guinness. That guard seemed friendlier.

He then got more serious.

'Take off,' he said pointing to my rear pannier.

'Out,' he continued asking me to remove everything. I did so and sprayed my assortments all over the floor. For the next 20 minutes the guards went through everything and asked me what it was for.

'Why two toothbrush?'

'One for my teeth and the black one for my dirty chain?

'What this?'

'My bike tool.'

'What this do?' he said pointing at the chain link removal part in the bike tool.

'And this?' he said pointing at the spanner. This carried on. I had to describe everything, where I was going, how many kilometres I was cycling. How heavy my bike was. How much it cost. (I told them I borrowed it from a friend) Why was I on such thin tyres? Where was I sleeping at night? And so on. At one point he opened the bag with my stinking sleeping bag and quickly closed it and turned away in disgust and said something to the other guard. The other guard laughed, he did not.

'OK. Go there,' he said and pointed me to another window. Here I had more of the same questions about my journey before he stamped my passport and sent me on my way.

Was this it? Was I in Russia? I cycled about 100 metres in the dark before I came to another set of gates with another guard, this time in a different uniform. Ah, this was the Russian Border. The last bit was me just leaving the Ukraine. With all the fuss they made in me leaving, I only imagined what was about to happen to enter Russia.

I followed a similar path from guard to guard but no one wanted to check my bike this time. Eventually I got to what seemed to be the final window. After that there was nothing but darkness. The woman, who looked a bit like a man, looked at my passport and then looked at me with the scariest look I've ever seen.

'Visa finish. No enter Russia,' and she pointed to the page of my Visa. This couldn't be right. Had I got the dates wrong on my Visa application? I looked closely. No. It was the Russian Visa I had got for my previous failed attempt but seeing as I had never reached Russia it had never been stamped.

'No, other Visa,' I said and signalled for her to turn to another page. She did so and then went back to the outdated Visa.

'Why you no use?' she said.

'Well, um, you see I was meant to come to Russia but then got sick and couldn't come.'

She looked at me, back at my passport, back at me. Closed it and gave it back to me.

'No. Go wait in room,' she said and pointed to an over-lit fluorescent room behind her cabin.

I wheeled Miss Moneypenny around, left her against a railing and went and sat inside. There was no one in there but me. On the one side it looked like there were some sort of counters but the shutters were down to the floor in front of each one.

I sat there for half an hour before someone came in from a side door.

'Come,' he said. I followed. He took me down a long corridor and into a small side room. In there was a camera facing a chair.

'Sit,' he said. I did so. My heart was racing. I've never been in an interrogation room before and even though I knew I had done nothing wrong, I somehow already felt guilty of doing something.

His questions were similar to everyone else's as I explained the world record, how far I'd cycled and how I was very much looking forward to the best part of the ride, Russia. He seemed happy with my answers and once or twice even gave a smile but then the part of his training that said; do not smile, ever, forced him to over theatrically frown again.

'OK. Welcome to Russia,' he said and gave me my passport back and took me back to Miss Moneypenny. I then went back to the same lady who just stamped my passport and sent me to the final booth. I got there and there was a man with a dog. He looked at me and the dog straight away went and sniffed Pedro.

Bollocks! Pedro. I had completely forgotten about Pedro and hadn't covered him up. I can't believe the Ukraine chap wanted to know why I had two toothbrushes but hadn't noticed Pedro. I thought back and I then remembered I had hung my helmet over the front of the aero bars. It must have covered him up. I was now wearing the helmet and Pedro was in full view and now this guard and his dog, probably Pedro's cousin, were very interested.

'What is this?' he said.

This was not good. There was no scenario where this would end well for us. Even if I was let go without rubber glove treatment, Pedro's adventure was now surely over. That made me so sad. We had come so far together. He had been my whip, cracking it whenever I felt weak and wanted to give up. Now he'd land up being incinerated or something.

'I found it just there,' I said and pointed as if I had just picked it up, which hopefully would be less of a sentence. Hopefully Russia thought of Ukrainian dogs as less 'infected' than dogs from further afield, like Spain.

The man then looked up and shouted something to another guard, who looked like his boss, and then pointed at Pedro. That boss guard was busy with a truck driver and ignored him.

He shouted again and pointed at Pedro. This time the boss looked up. He started walking over. This was it.

'I'm so sorry Pedro,' I said under my breath.

Then suddenly something was said on the loud speaker. The boss immediately turned and started walking fast back towards the interrogation building. The dog guard then looked at me and shook his head.

'Go!' he said angrily and waved me through.

Was I really through? Had Pedro and I made it into Russia? It had only taken about 3 hours but it looked like we were in. I looked ahead for any other signs of a building but it was pitch dark. I decided to cycle out of ear shot before I stopped and said at the top of my voice.

'We've made it Pedro. We're in Russia. Only 1,200 miles to go.'

The final leg was just about to begin. A few miles away I found some shelter under a few trees opposite a row of houses. I set my alarm for half an hour before sunrise so that I could leave before anyone saw me.

More incredible buildings in Russia

Race Time: 17 Days. 9 Hours. 20 Minutes
Location: Kozino, Russia
Miles Cycled: 2886

Other than some dogs barking, I had one of my better night's sleep. This was mostly due to my clean clothes which I had decided to sleep in as it was a bit cooler overnight. What lay before me was daunting and terrifying. 1,200 miles of what will most certainly be the most challenging of sections. I kept repeating Rory's saying to me, 'No one wants to run over a cyclist.' Even though I was saying it, it was hard to ignore the glaring facts about Russian roads and traffic deaths. This worry was made glaringly obvious when the first car I saw, still in the pitch dark, didn't have its lights on.

'No one gets run over twice, and I've had my turn,' I kept adding to the end of Rory's quote.

The morning light came and Russia presented itself in all its glory. Colourful mosaic bus stops and similarly designed houses flanked the roads as people saddled up their donkeys for a hard day's graft. I had been ignored for most of Europe other than a few extra head nods from the Czech Republic onwards. In Russia however, I suddenly became something very foreign. Something that made people want to stare at me with the same old questioning eyes. I was from somewhere far way. Also I presume you don't get many ginger people in Russia, but this turned out to be a misconception. There is a part of Russia that has the same percentage of ginger people as Scotland. I promised myself I'd go there one day.

As with each new country I had no money and again the ATM tried to rip me off with the minimum I could withdraw being £400 unless I pushed 'other amount.' Luckily, I was now wise to the worldly misdoings of rogue ATMs. It did however take me 30 miles to find breakfast and after skipping the dinner at the border I was starved. Breakfast landed up being dried fish and crisps while I became reacquainted with my long-lost friend, the long drop, before remembering there was a good reason we'd not remained close. At least the loo roll I had carried all the way from Portugal was finally being put to good use thus making my set-up an extra 20g lighter.

I always knew the roads would be bad in Russia but I hadn't quite expected just how terrible they were. The only way to achieve decent mileage was to cycle on the motorways, which is allowed in Russia, stupidly, and I have no idea why. They are horrific. Most motorways in Russia are just two lanes wide, one each way. There is no hard shoulder at all. They're basically the same as B roads in Britain but long and straight. The only difference is there is about 3m of dirt on the side of the road for trucks that break down or for people who need a pee, or vomit from too much Vodka.

It soon became clear that the road was definitely not wide enough for two trucks and a cyclist. Dangerously not wide enough at all. This meant that whenever there was a truck coming towards me in the opposite lane, and one overtaking me, I had to move over into the dirt, sometimes coming to a complete stop, waiting for the trucks to pass, and then remounting the road and continuing, having lost all my momentum. It was exhausting. I spent most of the day looking in my mirrors and as a result missed potholes which eventually resulted in me getting another pinch flat. I swapped the tube for a fresh one and pushed on. Along with playing chicken with trucks all day I had a 15mph headwind, literally bang on the nose. There were no trees, no corners, and no shelter from my cycle computer screaming up at me that I was only doing 8 miles per hour.

By 2pm, having been on the road for nearly 10 hours I had only managed to cycle 85 miles. To make matters worse it looked like I was due to have headwinds for the next week, all the way to Ufa, over 1,000 miles away.

Service stations weren't great nutritionally either, unless vodka counted, in which case there was an abundance of choice. My meals mostly consisted of packets of crisps and various dried meats for protein which included rabbit, horse, pig and the seemingly mundane beef. The one thing that kept me amused somewhat in my turmoil of headwinds was that one station was playing Wham's 'Last Christmas.' They obviously don't know the unwritten social protocol of only being allowed to play Christmas songs in December and December only.

In an effort to not let the wind get to me I was taking great pleasure in appreciating all the old Lada cars in various stages of disrepair. One of these beauties overtook me and about a mile later was pulled up on the side of the road with its bonnet up. The driver, an old chap, was adding water to the radiator. I waved and he nodded. 10 minutes later he overtook me and we shared a smile and a nod. An hour later I passed him again on the side of the road with the bonnet up again. This time he was just waiting for something to cool down I guessed. This happened for the next 4 hours as I overtook him 5 times, each time he'd say something to me and kind of roll his eyes back. It must have been rather annoying for him to be constantly overtaken by a bicycle but he remained in good spirits none the less. This weirdly lifted my mood. He had a car with a leaky radiator and there was nothing he could do about it except stop whenever it overheated and wait a while. Yet he seemed happy. I had terrible truck-ridden roads with a stonking headwind, something I too could do nothing about. I still had a day on Jonas, and Johan was probably also having issues with this wind too. I just needed to put my head down and stay upbeat.

My head was down so much that I nearly missed the fact I had reached 3,000 miles. I pulled over and opened another one of Caroline's letters. I didn't cry this time either but instead was inspired to push harder. I was so close to the end now I could almost smell it. At the end would be Caroline, Millie and Shackleton, and our wedding. That was definitely something to inspire me to get to Ufa quicker. I got back on Miss Moneypenny feeling happy.

My new positive mind-set lasted all of 10 minutes when a truck snuck up on me while I was looking at my maps and hooted right next to my head giving me the fright of my life and sending me off the road and down the bank. How I managed to stay upright I'll never know. It was getting dark and the idea of cycling on these roads at night seemed a death wish. Not even the Bradley Wiggle was working out here. I had only done 147 miles, another short day, but day 1 in a new country was always going to be slow. My lead had dropped to 23 hours. I had lost 3 hours to Jonas in 1 day. Tomorrow I'd smash it. I kept telling myself.

To try and claw back minutes I decided to sleep right near the road and not go down a side road which took a few minutes longer. Luckily I found pretty much the closest place I could to the road in the form of a drain pipe which ran under the road, and it was dry. Drainpipes are one of my favourite places to camp. They are surprisingly quiet. You're completely out of sight from the road and they provide shelter from the dew. The one downside is that other creatures often use them too, like frogs, rats and wolves. I was willing to take the risk for a good night's sleep though. If I was intending to attack tomorrow, I'd need the rest.

Puncture hell

Race Time: 18 Days. 9 Hours. 0 Minutes
Location: Timskyi, Russia
Miles Cycled: 3037

I was up early, earlier than the truck drivers. I had the best night's sleep outside of hotels all ride. Even having to blow up my camping mat twice and losing an ear-plug didn't bother me. I searched everywhere for the damn ear-plug but resigned myself to the fact it fell out and a rat ate it. I still had enough in the one ear to split in half for the rest of the ride. I felt in good spirits. I was dry, hadn't been eaten by a wolf and would get some good miles in before the truck drivers awoke from their vodka slumbers.

In spite of getting food within a mile of camping, all hopes of an attack day were obliterated when the wind picked up, even stronger than yesterday. 20 miles per hour, on the nose again. The invisible army of doom battering my face.

I stopped again at around 2pm for a second lunch and two things happened. The first was that I found my lost ear-plug lodged in my beard. I can't tell you how much this amused me and lifted my spirits. To think I had cycled all morning and it had been stuck there.

The second thing was, a police officer carrying an Uzi machine gun and riot helmet, stormed the service station. Everyone froze. He just stood there in the doorway in some sort of western saloon entrance pose, all backlit and powerful, except he wasn't. He was small and thin and the fluorescent light hardly added any sense of grandeur. He then shouted something to the attendant, smiled, held the machine gun up to him, pointed at it, laughed, and said something to which the attendant laughed back. He then walked back outside, opened the boot of his Opel(Vauxhall) Astra Hatchback, used the baton to keep the boot open and took his riot helmet and armoured vest off. He then waved the Uzi back at the attendant, and drove off. From the looks of things, the policeman just wanted to show off to his friend that he was now in possession of a machine gun and could kill people if he wanted. Oh, the joker he was. Everyone else in the service station just carried on with whatever they were doing as if this kind of thing happened all the time.

The headwinds continued to batter me all day. I cycled up long slow hills, spending half the time in the dirt and the other half swearing repeatedly at truck drivers for totally ignoring my Bradley Wiggle. It's as if running over a cyclist was just a mild inconvenience in a 'I shouldn't have been cycling on the road anyway' mentality. Jonas was catching me by the hour and there was nothing I could do about it. It seemed he had a tailwind on this section. I've had a beard since 2012 and have never once thought of shaving but today was the closest I have come to buying a razor, convinced the extra drag would make me lose the record.

Nothing much happened for the rest of the day and I eventually ended on a dismal 155 miles. My lead was down to 19 hours.

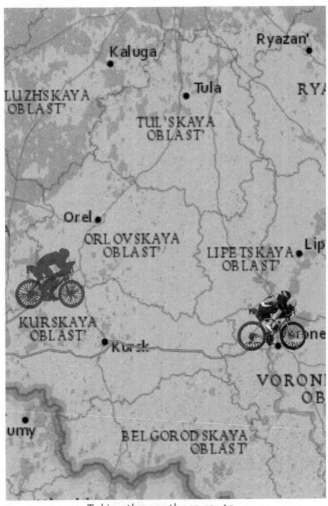

Taking the southern route

Race Time: 19 Days. 9 Hours. 0 Minutes
Location: Anninskiy, Russia
Miles Cycled: 3192

The good thing about Sundays was that the roads were pretty quiet for most of the morning. This was a welcomed break after the last few days of hell. The downside, as always, is nothing opens for food. Today, however, seemed to be the exception as I found a 24 hour roadside café. I had seen these signs a few times before but I thought they were hotels. The menus were far better than service stations, so at 5am I ordered macaroni and chicken, and ordered it again 10 minutes later to the bemusement of the waitress who was actually quite friendly and keen to practice her English. She taught me some Russian too, which I immediately forgot of course.

It felt like I was slowly getting into the swing of Russia. I now knew where to get better food and the second decision I made was that whenever two trucks came past me (one in each direction), I would simply HAVE to move into the dirt, no questions. Up till now I was constantly making loads of calculations based on my observation in my rear-view mirrors. How wide was the road? How fast was the truck going? Were they moving over at all and if so by how much? Would I still have room? How wide and when I should do my Bradley Wiggle? Only after I had done all these calculations, would I decide whether or not to move into the dirt or just stay in the road, but move my head away from deadly head height wing-mirrors. It was exhausting doing this every minute or so. Now that I had made the rule that I HAD to move over, it freed up so much more brain space for other things like finding better food, stretching more and looking around to enjoy the scenery. It really did work and my mood was instantly lifted, even though my mileage suffered. But I calculated roughly I should still remain ahead. I think.

By midday and another wolf roadkill later, people seemed to be waking up and going about their Sunday business which wasn't that dissimilar to anyone else's. Some dressed up for church. Others were going on Sunday strolls and I even passed a car boot sale. It took every ounce of willpower not to stop. Imagine I lost the record because I had stopped at a car boot sale to look at Russian lampshades and knackered hedge-trimmers.

Not only was I losing time to the wind, but today I just couldn't find my rhythm at all. I seemed to be stopping every hour to do things that really didn't need doing. Tying my shoelaces tighter, then a mile later loosening them again. Stopping to clean the gunk out of my chain. Moving my saddle backwards because my arse hurt. This was happening a lot, my arse hurting. The saddle sores were here for good and what I really needed was a new pair of shorts but didn't hold out much hope of finding any.

It was hot too, somewhere near the 30's Celsius I guessed and the hot headwind felt like I was standing in front of a fan heater all day. My liquid intake was already about 10 litres per day but probably needed to be around 15 to keep hydrated.

By 8pm I had only done 145 miles and it was getting dark and one of the sores on my backside bruised heavily on a pothole I hit while concentrating on a truck that seemed intent on running me over. For the last hour I had to get off the saddle every few minutes to relieve the pain. I decided to take Ibuprofen to help, something I don't like doing as it would now mask my VMO twinge, still bothering me, albeit not as much as my arse. If I put too much pressure through my VMO because it felt good I could further injure it. But I decided to risk it. My backside needed it.

I found another drainpipe to camp in and set my alarm for 3.58am again. Jonas was now 17 hours behind me and gaining on me fast.

Drainpipe camp spot

Race Time: 20 Days. 8 Hours. 58 Minutes
Location: Balashov, Russia
Miles Cycled: 3337

Another good night's sleep but any thoughts of attack quickly disappeared again when I hit the road and right back into the headwind. No matter how many times I refreshed the Windfinder website, it still said I was to have headwinds all the way to Ufa. Tired and weak, with a sore arse and a slightly lame leg, I limped on at 8 miles per hour. The only good thing that happened was a service station a mile from my drain pipe, so I was able to get a huge packet of processed croissants.

5 miles later I hit a rock. It was still dark which made repairing my tyre rather hard. I had run out of new inners and the other two in my bag had holes in too, so I repaired the one I had in the front tyre and continued.

While I was doing the 300 pumps to get the tyre to a decent pressure, a car did a rather aggressive U-turn and came screeching up next to me. I was actually too tired to care. The man rushed out and said something in Russian. I looked at him and just said.

'Flat tyre. Fix.'

'Oh, OK,' he said in broken English.

'Welcome in Russia,' he continued before getting back in his car. He then did a doughnut in the road and zoomed off again. It was strange interacting with someone outside of service stations. Most people, since the start in Portugal, hadn't seemed overly excited about life, but then I guess service station attendants at 4am aren't the best example to judge the general enthusiasm of a nation. The doughnut driver, who seemed to be coming to my rescue, was a good example of that.

It seemed today was the day for people to stop me because at around 10am someone else drove past, hooted, pulled up a few hundred metres away and jumped out his car waving a water bottle. I gladly accepted it as I was low on my new daily target of 15 litres, something I never once reached.

He spoke no English but all he really wanted to tell me was how he was speaking to truck drivers in Bulgaria on his CB radio. His car had three huge antennae sticking out of the roof; one must have been 2 metres high if not more. He then got back in his car, said something on his CB radio, smiled at me and drove off leaving me in a cloud of dust. Friendly chap at least. I downed the 500ml water there and then and sucked the air out of the bottle to crush it down small enough to fit in my back pocket.

My route headed northwest of Saratov, through some more built up back streets with tar roads that were so potholed, drivers were choosing to drive on the dirt on the side of the road. Neither was good for me. I was either swerving in and out or slowing to a near stop through all the potholes in the tar, or getting covered in dust and having to move out the way of cars bombing along the dirt.

I dodged the potholes for another 2 hours before my luck ran out and I got another flat. Annoyingly it seemed that I just hadn't fixed my previous puncture properly and the air pushed its way out the side of the self-stick patch. To save time I just decided to put another self-stick over the exit hole and carried on. I just needed to get out of town, fast.

Finally, something was working out for me. At the north end of Saratov I came across a Decathlon store. Just what I needed for a new pair of shorts. I dashed in and took a pair that looked like they may fit, paid for them and ran to the changing rooms to put them on. I removed my current shorts for the first time in the day light and nearly gagged. The stench along with flakes of skin were all too much. I put the new ones on and they felt incredible. The padding was however not that thick, so I regrettably decided to put the old ones back over the new ones. It felt strange to walk in, but getting back on Miss Moneypenny made me realise it had been a good plan. Anything to help my saddle sores from the battering they were getting.

10 miles later my front tyre went flat again and the joys of a slightly more comfortable arse all but disappeared. I knew it was the dodgy patch so got out one of the other punctured inner tubes in my bag and decided to fix that

one. Strange I thought. It seemed rather thin. I read 'For 18-23c tyres'. This was not good. I had 28c tyres. There was no way a patch would stay on the 18c tube because the amount it would have to stretch to expand into the 28c tyre would make the patch come loose. I put it away and looked for the last remaining inner. What? It too was 18-23c. How had I got this so wrong? Then I remembered. About 6 months previously I had swapped 23c tyres for the 28cs and I hadn't swapped the tubes. This was a disaster. If I couldn't fix the 28c tubes, of which I only had two, then it could be game over. Even if I found a bike shop it would be hard to find 60mm presta valves to fit my deep section rims. It seems unimaginable to think that I could lose this record because I had the wrong size inner tubes. I'd never forgive myself.

I reverted back to the original tube and added 3 more patches completely smothering any chance of air escaping. Another 300 pumps and sore shoulders later, I continued. I managed another 20 miles or so before I heard the unmistakeable sound of air escaping. How could 5 patches have not worked. I stopped on the side of the road and decided to remove them all and start again, this time with a glue patch, like the old school days. The problem was that when I removed the self-stick ones, they left a bit of themselves on the tube. A sticky residue that wouldn't harden and I couldn't sand off. I had no idea if my glue patch would stick to this, but I gave it a go anyway. I waited 15 minutes for it to dry and then put another 8 self-stick patches all around the main one just in case, this time being as careful as ever to press them flat to minimise any escape.

The 300 pumps took another 10 minutes as my shoulders burned inside, especially my left one which is still pretty weak after my Gloucester Cheese Rolling tumble of 2009. Eventually up and running again I hit the road. I had lost 2 hours with buying my new shorts and punctures and another 3 or so hours due to headwinds. I could almost smell Jonas steaming up behind me. It was not good.

I think it was 10pm when I finally decided to finish for the day. It could actually have been 11pm as I was still due 2 time zone changes and didn't know if I had gone through one. I had only done 130 miles and decided to camp up under a bridge. The ground was rocky but at least it was dry. For the next few days I'd be cycling northeast along the Volga River before turning directly east and joining up with the same route as Jonas for the last few days. I was still ahead but not by much. One spoke break or other mechanical and that would be me, out of contention.

Feeling deflated from days of headwinds

Race Time: 21 Days. 7 Hours. 30 Minutes
Location: Sinodskoe, Russia
Miles Cycled: 3467

I had the worst night's sleep with my mat deflating three times and my hips getting battered by the sharp rocks on the floor. What made the sleep even worse was that on the 3rd time I rolled over to blow up my sodding mat, I saw, by the light of the moon, I had somehow managed to miss a human turd lying about 30cm from my head. There wasn't much room to move away from it so I just rolled over and tried to put it out my mind, which of course was impossible; it was a human turd next to my head after all.

It seems having a steaming pile next to your head all night has a somewhat adverse effect on your day. A step up from getting out the wrong side of the bed. I just couldn't find my rhythm again. It seemed Miss Moneypenny too had had enough. Her gears were starting to slip now and then. This was because I should have changed her chain at around 2,000 miles but chose not to. The chain was now so over-stretched it didn't quite fit around the cassette. I also seemed to have a clicking in the rear wheel when I was going slowly. Something had broken off inside the rim and was bouncing around. I deduced it could be one of two things. It could be one of the spoke nipples that had broken off. I stopped and squeezed each spoke to see if any were loose. They were all solid. This left an even potentially more worrying scenario. It could have been a bit of the rim itself that had broken off, hitting one of the many potholes I have hit since I got these wheels 15,000 miles ago, which could have resulted in a hairline fracture on the inside. A total wheel failure was then very likely. With the record so close to the bone if this happened it would be game over for me, not to mention the dangers of crashing on Russian roads. The thoughts of falling in front of a truck because of a buckled wheel sent shivers down my spine. This was just another straw that was slowly breaking my back on top of the pulled VMO, monstrous headwinds, saddle sores, speeding truck drivers and poor food and sleep. Russia was throwing everything at me and it seemed I was at breaking point. I felt an overwhelming heaviness all over my body and mind, and for most of the day I didn't lift my gaze further than a few metres in front of me.

By early evening I had only cycled 127 miles but I had nothing left in the tank. Jonas had done somewhere in the region of 160 miles. Yet another dismal day with the record slipping away from me. At one point I was going so slowly that I worked out even if I cycled for 24 hours a day I'd get to Ufa 3 hours after Jonas.

I found a truck stop with dorm rooms and managed to get a dorm to myself which is what I needed. I just wanted to be alone. I ate two meals, had another date with a long drop and tucked myself into bed before it was even dark. I struggled to work out why I was finding this last section so hard. Even now as I write this it's hard to explain. Lack of fitness perhaps. This was certainly true. I wasn't nearly as fit as I had hoped to be. 3 weeks of sleep deprivation undoubtedly added to the situation. But I think most of all, and it's annoyingly the reason that sounds the silliest, but I think it was the brutal headwind that I was constantly fighting, constantly seeing my speedometer in single figures, constantly watching as Jonas was catching me. That worry alone was enough to ruin anyone's spirits. Even Pedro turned from a fictional character to banter with, to a dead weight slowing me down. My mind was not in a good place. I thought about crying as I lay on the bottom bunk in the cold cabin but tears wouldn't come. I was just too deeply and utterly fatigued.

Keeping focused on the end

Race Time: 22 Days. 8 Hours. 0 Minutes
Location: Syzran, Russia
Miles Cycled: 3594

I slept for a solid 8 hours, the longest sleep I had had in 3 weeks. I was still in deep fatigue but less sleepy now, which helped a bit. The first 5 miles were all downhill towards Syzran where I managed to get an early breakfast. I felt strangely good. Maybe today was the day to attack?

The wind was still bang on the nose but the better sleep and early breakfast made up for it. I pushed hard all day. I was now back on the same route as Jonas and if I stayed on the current projection of dismal mileage I would potentially be only 2 hours ahead of him by the time I reached Ufa. It was coming down to the wire. I desperately needed a 170 mile plus day to ease the pressure from the last 36 hours.

Russia continued to throw everything at me. The roads progressively got worse and at times I just chose to cycle in the dirt on the side of the highway for miles, just to rest my brain from the constant worry of being run over.

I kept my head down all day, not taking anything in, just trying to tuck myself into the smallest of balls to cut through the wind. I even put my hands in a prayer form on the front of my bars. This I hoped would cut through the air better, anything to gain miles.

It must have worked because I managed 165 miles, my biggest day in nearly a week. It's just what I needed and I settled into another truck stop motel and passed out.

First sign for Ufa

Race Time: 23 Days. 12 Hours. 0 Minutes
Location: Sukhodol, Russia
Miles Cycled: 3759

This was it. I had 36 hours to get to Ufa. Jonas was 8 hours behind me now. In the last 5 days I had lost about 18 hours to him.

The morning was bitterly cold as I left the warmth of the motel. Annoyingly the first mile was downhill which cut to the bone. Ideally you want an uphill first thing in the morning to get your legs working and warmed up. I couldn't have gone more than 500 metres when I heard the distinct sound of air leaving my tyre and then the unmistakable bump and grind as the rim hit the tarmac. This is not what I needed now. It was my rear tyre this time. I had been carrying a spare new tyre all the way from Portugal and always said the first puncture I got on the rear after halfway I'd swap the tyre over. I never got that puncture until now, 36 hours from the end. What's even more incredible is that the tyre wasn't new to start with. It already had about 500 miles on it before I started.

Finally the karma gods were in a good mood and there was a service station just ahead, so I got off and walked to it, ordered a coffee and some food before heading back out in the cold to patch the inner tube and put the new tyre on. I can't tell you how satisfying it was to get rid of the old tyre, making my setup another 200g lighter.

'Pedro. We're going to smash it now,' I found myself saying and then realised I hadn't chatted much to him in the last few days. Pedro was meant to be the silly, pointless mascot which added some 'fun' to my adventure but I had forgotten to make an effort to have 'fun'. Yes, the single act of cycling 18 hours a day, doing 8 miles per hour into a 20 mile an hour headwind, dodging trucks centimetres from your head, I can assure you, was not anywhere close to fun. Still, I was having an adventure across Europe and 36 hours away from a dream that was a decade in the making. I needed to remember that the worst day on my bike was still better than my best day as a grumpy school portrait photographer. Falling into the wonderful world of nostalgia I completely missed the fact a driver coming in from a side road hadn't seen me and pulled right in front of me. I swerved behind him but he stopped too. I was heading right for his door. I could see the panic in his eyes. Luckily I hadn't been on my aero bars and was able to hit the brakes hard and stopped just short of the rear door. The elderly driver seemed really embarrassed and just sped off to avoid confrontation. I'm kind of glad he did as I didn't have the energy for an argument anyway.

I carried on cycling and heard that rear wheel clicking was getting worse.

'Please, please, please just last till tomorrow, please,' I said out loud, pleading with Miss Moneypenny to stay in one piece for the last day and a half.

I managed to keep a steady pace all day and again didn't move my gaze away from the road ahead, scouring the road for any bump, rock or pothole that could break my rear wheel.

I was nearing the Ural Mountains and climbing slowly. The evening got colder but I pushed hard. I wanted to have less than 100 miles to do on the final day. By midnight I passed another motel and the draw was too strong. It was bitterly cold, too cold for my sleeping bag. I always knew this last section would be cold and I always planned to stay in hotels, or ride the night through depending on how much of a lead I had. I still had a 7-hour lead and knew that Jonas had one more sleep than me still to do which afforded me a good 4 hours rest so that I wouldn't have to cycle on Russian roads at night. There was no point in risking it just to gain more hours on him. I was playing it safe which I hoped I'd not regret.

The final push to the end

Race Time: 24 Days. 6 Hours. 0 Minutes
Location: Novosukkulovo, Russia
Miles Cycled: 3865

I dreamt about breaking a wheel all night and hardly slept. I kept thinking I should have just carried on cycling to get further in the lead. I still had a lead of course, 6 hours or so. Not exactly a comfortable lead as one spoke break or tyre wall split could end it for me but at least I was still ahead and only had 120 odd miles left to cycle.

I made the most of the quieter, windless morning as the sun rose, warming me up. I looked around for the first time in a while. Russia was vast, scary and unrelenting in its quest to slow me down. As far as I could see there was nothing. Just farmlands and the occasional nodding donkey quietly working away. I took my headphone out and listened to the morning. I ignored the pain in my legs.

I ignored the clicking wheel and the skipping chain. I ignored the fatigue, the stress hormones that had built up in my body. Instead I began thinking about all the highs and lows I've endured and celebrated over the years. Constantly falling over my handlebars as a child. Freezing my hands off cycling Britain in winter. That daunting feeling when I sold my business for £1 to cycle around the world. Getting run over in America. Getting looked after by the wonderful Martin and Missy Carey. All the injuries and failed attempts. Sunrises and sunsets, punctures and pedal strokes and free cups of tea. Big mile cycling changed my life and I'm aware I will probably only truly realise the change much later in life. But I liked that. I wasn't in a rush for it all to make sense straight away.

Before I knew it, I came over the last horizon and saw the vastness of Ufa in the distance. My eyes started to well up. It was a strange feeling cycling those last few miles. As I approached the finish point, a statue high up on the edge of a hill, I started to realize my dream was now actually going to come true. There were no fans. No adoring crowds throwing flowers or underpants. No media. No pomp and ceremony. I didn't need the fanfare. I didn't need to jump for joy. I was jumping for joy inside. I reached the statue and Miss Moneypenny felt immediately heavy so I laid her down and sat on the pavement. It was all over.

Struggling to keep my eyes open, full of tears, it hit me, hard. I had just achieved a dream that had taken me over 10 years and 60,000 miles battling deserts, tornados, blizzards and every other hardship imaginable. It has been the most testing years of my life. All in pursuit of two dreams, the dream of trying to break a cycling world record, and the dream of completing the third and final F in endurance – a world's fastest. In reaching Ufa in a time of 24 days, 16 hours and 55 minutes, I had finally completed both. I had nothing left to give. The only thing I felt like doing was lying down, and going to sleep.

I remembered Lee saying; 'I just aint happy when I'm not riding.' and Mike saying; 'You can't take yourself too seriously. It's just riding bicycles at the end of the day.'

Thank you both for making me believe again. Making me believe that just riding my bicycle was enough, and in that belief, you helped me fulfil my dreams.

Ride in peace my friends.

Sean

The end

EPILOGUE

An hour passed once I had called Caroline and told her I had done it. Friends and family were all congratulating me and my sister was especially concerned that I would miss my flight to South Africa for her wedding in a few days' time. Something was bothering me though and I didn't know what it was. I suddenly remembered something in the Guinness rules about the ending. It hadn't mentioned this statue as the official finish point. I quickly searched my emails for the application which had a PDF with the rules.

It read: *The record attempt must start at the Ufa Railway Terminal, Russia and finish at the lighthouse at Cabo de Roca, Portugal (or* vice versa*).*

'Bollocks Pedro,' I shouted and picked up Miss Moneypenny who weighed a tonne. The statue wasn't the official end point. I got my maps out and saw that I was still half an hour from the station. I pedalled as fast as I could before eventually reaching the entrance where I stopped and took a selfie to prove I was there. My new final official time being: 24 days, 18 hours and 39 minutes - 8 hours ahead of Jonas.

I chuckled to myself at the idea that I may have flown home having not officially completed the ride. I would then have to do it all over again.

Was I now one of those 'big mile cyclists' that'll be talked about for centuries to come? Of course not. Most of the cyclists I mention in this book would easily be able to beat my record, but that doesn't bother me. This journey has been a personal one. A voyage of self-discovery, a monumental quest to gain confidence and life experience I would never have got had I carried on doing something I hated, purely for the money. It's hard to explain the feeling you get when reaching something that has taken so long to achieve. We're all caught up in an ever-speeding world where rapid success is revered and people often feel less of themselves if they too don't find 'success' quickly. But the truth is, no one is 'successful' overnight. Everyone who has achieved something great will undoubtedly have been through a lot of pain and hardship to get there, it's just no one knew about it until they had achieved it.

I also never found out about Johan. In fact, I had somewhat forgotten about him until I was sitting in the airport the next day. I searched online but as with the news nowadays my story was already everywhere. Headlines read; Extreme adventurer Sean Conway breaks Europe cycle record. Extreme? I laughed. I didn't feel extreme at all. I felt skinny, tired and desperate for a comfortable night's sleep.

As I boarded the flight leaving Russia an overwhelming sense of pride and achievement came over me. My eyes started to well up. It really was over. I really had done it. The only real question now was, what's next?

The actual official end – Ufa train station

THE FUTURE

Big mile races like the TCR, TransAm, Tour Divide and other records like across Europe are getting more and more popular. In fact TCR is oversubscribed which means people can't just rock up and join the flash mob anymore like they used too. They are becoming bigger, more commercial, getting primetime media coverage and some of the winners, the ones who actively try, are getting sponsorship deals. The likes of Mark Beaumont, Juliana Buhring and Julian Sayarer to name a few have written very good books, which people buy and many will go on to do motivational speaking about their achievement, much like an Olympian would. In the last few years this pot of big mile cyclists who've managed to kind of make it somewhat of a 'career', and I do mean it in the loosest term, (for the most part there is still no financial reward for these riders) is getting bigger. I'm a classic example of that I guess.